Analyzing Social Problems through Mindful Spiritual Stories

Dr. Yunus Kumek

Sage Chronicle λ
publishing house

Interior images selected by T. Hajdaj from Pixabay
Cover image by Yunus Kumek

Sage Chronicle $^{\lambda}$
publishing house
www.sagechronicle.org
3380 Sheridan Drive, #240
New York 14226
contact@sagechronicle.org

CONTENTS

PREFACE

This book examines and analyzes our social problems through daily spiritual and practical mindful stories in different contexts. This book is an especially useful supplementary text in the fields of sociology of religion, psychology of religion, religion, philosophy, and contemporary religious thoughts.

Yunus Kumek, PhD
Harvard Divinity School
Fall 2019

Analyzing Social Problems through Mindful Spiritual Stories

1. The Upside Down Bug

One day, Daniel was walking with his kids. There were a lot of bugs. As they were walking, he was thinking. Then, Daniel saw a bug upside down struggling to get right side up. He continued walking. After walking for a mile, he felt something uneasy in himself. He said to himself, "What is happening?" Then, he thought about the bug and realized he should have helped it. He went back and after a few minutes of searching, he found the bug in the same spot where he initially saw it and it was still struggling to change its position. Daniel helped it to re-orient itself and get back on its feet again. He felt much better and left.

IN PRACTICE

It is important to detect one's spiritual problems, and then diagnose and treat them accordingly. A lot of times, the person may not know the cause of spiritual discomfort, uneasiness, fear, anxiety, or distress. The person can make the problem worse by ignoring it or treating it the wrong way. Therefore, in practice the famous saying 'Know yourself to know God' alludes to this notion. In the above story, perhaps Daniel was distracted while thinking and walking with his kids. When he glanced at the bug, he did not internalize this creation's pain. But the image stuck in his memory and transformed into a discomfort in himself. Later, as Daniel thought and reflected on his discomfort, he then interpreted that the source of distress was his unconcerned attitude towards the suffering bug.

Discussion Question

▶ How can a person practice greater awareness of their inner conversations?

2. The External, the Internal, and the Purpose

One day, it was dark and rainy outside. Ben went to a social fitness club. As soon as he went inside, everyone was so cheerful. The lighting in the building was so bright. People were drinking coffee and enjoying their conversations in every corner. Everyone looked well dressed, happy, and was smiling. Then, he thought about his solitude, loneliness, and silence. He was then reflecting on moments in the temple, or in different places of meditation. Then, he asked himself, "What is the difference?" He said to himself, "This is the external. I do not know how these people are when they are with themselves in silence, which is the internal, the real self, and the purpose."

IN PRACTICE

It is important to know that the internal engagements are the essence that determine one's purpose in life. This does not mean the person should be in gloomy environments to engage with oneself with prayers, chants, reflection, and self-accountability. The person can use all of the means that would help with the real purpose whether being in nature or in different environments. As in the above story, on a smaller scale, a person can be happy in a nice social club with all of the cheerful, fine people. One should know that the universe itself is a social club if one understands how to engage with it. In other words, we are given a system

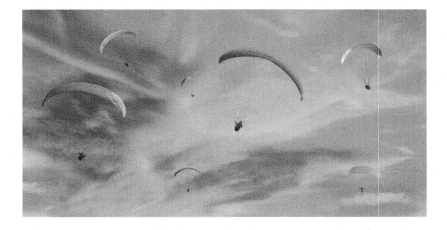

and structure populated with beings. Everyone is cheering, chanting, and appreciating their position with God. In this sense, a person not recognizing this disposition with God, may not have a real purpose although he or she may look happy. In the real state of solitude and self-reflection, there may be enormous internal spiritual bleeding such as depression, anxiety, and unhappiness.

Discussion Question

▶   What is your real self?

3. Friend or Companion

One day, Emma was thinking about the difference between the words 'friend' and 'companion'. She said to herself, "I think 'companion' is the person with whom you hang around. 'Friend' is a person with whom you go beyond companionship and develop a closer relationship."

IN PRACTICE

It is important to choose with whom one should hang around because the presence of others and their conversation can affect the person's spirituality positively or negatively. Therefore, the people who were around the prophets were called companions. They were with the prophets as much as possible to receive the constant positive spiritual flow into their hearts and minds. In other words, the words 'conversation' and 'companion' are from the same root word. In this relationship, the Friend does not leave the person and will always be there if the person is fulfilling the requirements of this relationship.

Discussion Question

▶ How do you contemporize the understanding of friend and companion during our times?

4. Balancing Ascetic Life and Social Life

One day, Jacob was enjoying his prayer. He was taking so much pleasure from it. As he was praying, his mom called him for assistance for a minute. Jacob immediately stopped his prayer and went next to his mom. His mom was happy with him. Jacob said to himself, "Although I was enjoying my prayer and it was very hard for me to break it, if God would be pleased, I would do it."

IN PRACTICE

The ascetic life through prayers, meditation, and solitude is encouraged with checks and balances. The full asceticism or monasticism through disconnecting oneself fully with their familial and social responsibilities is discouraged by the prophets. In other words, one can practice solitude or limited retreats with the intention of benefitting oneself, but then going back to people is considered more beneficial. There are a lot of genuine religious teachers who prefer to not socialize, and rather enjoy their prayers and meditation of God in solitude. However, they still socialize due to the rights of others over them, such as family members or students. In the above story, one can see the case of a mother especially being a person with rights. Therefore, one is required to stop one's optional spiritual engagement if their mother is calling. As suggested by the prophets, there were pious individuals who did not fulfill these kinship and social relations and therefore, they were tested with trials and difficulties by God.

Discussion Question

▶   Is ascetic life rare during our times? Why?

5. Mother

One day, David was contemplating why his kids are more attached to their mom than they are to him. Then, he was thinking about all of the difficulties of the labor that his wife went through during childbirth. Then, she had the struggles of breastfeeding and suckling. She was constantly worried about them. David said to himself, "I think I understand. It is payback time."

IN PRACTICE

According to the practice, both parents-father and mother-have rights over their children. The children are expected to take care of them and be nice to them even at the ages and times of being grumpy. The practice puts special emphasis on children being extra nice to mothers. According to some interpretations of the prophets, mothers have three times more rights over children than the fathers. In addition, even though a person may not get along well with their parents, children are still expected to remain nice, gentle, and kind in their treatment of them to please God. This instruction is stated numerous times in both the scripture and sayings of the prophets [1].

Discussion Question

▶　What are the factors that affect parent–children relationship?

6. People from Different Cultures and Learning

William used to choose different people as friends from different cultures. He used to hang around each day with a person from a different culture: an American, an Indian, an African, a Turk, and an Arab. One of his friends realized this and asked for the reason. William said, "I learn something different and new from each of them. They all understand and practice being close to God similarly, but also differently."

IN PRACTICE

On the journey of the spiritual path, the person can benefit from different people with different perspectives. A person who may not have the complete knowledge, and yet can be strong in genuine practice and can bring different perspectives. A person who may know the knowledge, using the mind constantly but lacking in practice, can also bring different perspectives. Each culture can bring different embodiments of the same teachings of spirituality. From this perspective, it is a unique experience to learn the spiritual practice from different people with different cultures as mentioned in the above story. Genuinely similar values are embodied differently in different cultures.

Discussion Question

> ▶ Why do some people view cultural diversity as richness and some view it as a possible source of problem?

7. Elizabeth's Promotion

Elizabeth worked in a company. She wanted to talk to her boss about a promotion. Therefore, she was seeking a good and happy time to approach her boss. One day, right before Thanksgiving, she came and asked her boss for a promotion at work. Her boss was in a happy mood because of approaching Thanksgiving. Elizabeth got her promotion and said, "Thank you, God."

IN PRACTICE

God is always merciful, forgiving, and appreciates the person's repentance and gratitude. There are also special times when the mercy of God is extra showering on people. During these times, the prayers, requests, and needs are especially fulfilled by God.

Discussion Question

▶ What is the wisdom of having special times, hours, or days in religious practices?

8. The No Wife-No Life Man

There was a man in the temple who used to always come to Brandon and complain and say, "No wife, no life!" This man was not able to get married. He used to always complain about life, his brothers, and his poverty. It was the same story every day. As this man used to approach Brandon, Brandon used to pretend as if he was busy praying and reading the scripture. One day, there was another poor man sleeping in the temple. This time, No wife-No life came to Brandon again and said, "Look, if I had money and car, I could have helped this poor man. But I do not have anything. What can I do…?" Brandon felt bad and sad.

IN PRACTICE

It is important to sympathize with people even if it may become difficult at times. We do not know each person's real situation. Only God knows. One of the prayers that Sufis constantly ask from God is: "Oh God, show us the realities of the things." In other words, an evil-seeming something may be good for the person; and on the other hand, something good-seeming may be bad for the person in its true reality.

Discussion Question

► Is it easy or difficult to sympathize with people? Why?

9. Life, Pain, and Gain

One day, Jake saw an old man crying in the temple and praying. Jake knew the man. The man did not have any relatives or family. He was going to have major surgery the next day. Jake was holding himself hard not to cry about this scene. Then, Jake said to himself, "God is more merciful than me and everyone. There is a pain, but always gain if it is done with pure intention."

IN PRACTICE

Sometimes, the evil and sad-seeming incidents can break our hearts. Sometimes a memory or a bad experience can make our hearts contract. One should remember to turn every opportunity of pain, evil, or good-seeming incident into an avenue to increase one's relationship with God. This is the final and ultimate purposeful engagement that would pay us back in this world and after death. In the above story, the old man transformed his pain into a fruitful relationship of attachment and going back to God and crying. The prophets mention that the power of tears genuinely flow in relationship with God. The fire of hell cannot touch these eyes in the afterlife.

Discussion Question

▶ Why are tears very important in practice?

10. The Dispute

Mary had a dispute with her husband. She felt that she was right. She felt uneasy, as usual, and asked forgiveness from her husband. Then, she felt better and relaxed.

IN PRACTICE

It is important not to have any ill feelings towards another person. The prophets mention that one cannot enter Heaven until one removes these feelings from one's heart. From this perspective, Mary implemented this teaching and felt better.

Discussion Question

▶ How can carrying negative feelings for others hurt the holder of these feelings?

11. Justice or Just-Us

Matt once had a friend who used to work at the court. He told Matt about a day he was working at the court. A few lawyers were talking about a plaintiff and defendant. The plaintiff had a good lawyer, but the defendant was not able to afford a lawyer. The lawyers were chatting and one sarcastically said to the other, 'This defendant does not have a lawyer. He will see if it is the justice or just-us." Matt smiled but was very disturbed.

IN PRACTICE

In the evil rendering of life, one can remember that there are things that we can control and there are things we cannot control. Even if one cannot do anything about an injustice or oppressive attitude or action, one need not make oneself complicit, and it is natural to have a feeling of disgust against this evil as one can see in the reaction of Matt to the above case that occurred.

Discussion Question

▶ How can one shun oneself from siding with injustices even though the person may not have any power to affect a situation?

12. Disciplining for Different Levels

One day, Sarah was with her son. Her son used to jump around, make noises, and disturb others. Sarah was trying to gently and softly calm her son down. She was afraid that others would be annoyed. She said to herself, "It is very delicate to gauge people at different levels. Kids are kids—accepting them with their child-like behavior. On the other hand, adults are often annoyed with every noise, sound, and disturbance."

IN PRACTICE

It is very important to recognize everyone according to their level. If one expects something from a person of a different level, the person can possibly break one's heart and future spiritual and physical potential for growth.

Discussion Question

▶ How do we actualize understanding people with different age, gender, and ethnic identities?

13. The Patient

One day, Felicity visited a friend in the hospital. Her friend had cancer and had just had surgery. When Felicity saw her in the hospital, she felt deep pain and sadness. Although she can try to understand reasons beyond the situation, she still felt pain and disturbed as a human.

She then said to herself, "What can I do to remove this pain?" She decided to go to church and pray. She felt better with the engagement of prayers and discharge.

IN PRACTICE

In life, there are times when incidents can affect and disturb us more than others. One should always be prepared for these 'hard-hitting' incidents. If the person practices worship, prayers, and chants regularly, these investments can reimburse the person when disasters happen. In the above case, Felicity had an exit point by going to church—praying and being by herself and with God. If the person does not know how to exit from these moments, there can be potential negative energy that can hurt the person.

Discussion Question

> ▶ How can one develop a spiritual mechanism to cope with evil-seeming and good-seeming incidents?

14. Harshness and Teaching

One day, Bianca invited a friend to her home. Her friend was a nice lady, but she believed in discipline and a little bit of harshness in the upbringing of kids. Bianca's kids knew the friend. As soon as she came, all of the kids were scared and behaving well. Bianca was thinking, "Which one is better? A display of softness, but sometimes the outcome of bad treatment by the kids? Or discipline with a little bit of harshness, but no outcome of bad treatment from the kids?"

IN PRACTICE

The ideal is to treat everyone—especially the kids—with a kind, gentle, and loving attitude. The prophets as the role model was the peak in this trait. The women, children, and everyone were very comfortable around the prophets. On the other hand, there are some teachers in the practice that they believe that the notion of discipline should also entail some fear to stop the bad behavior so that there is respect. During our times of changing values, the latter approach with discipline is getting more criticism. The discipline and respect have been implemented differently historically than in our times.

Discussion Question

 ▶   How do you understand cultures in child-parent and student-teacher relationships?

15. Changing Personalities

One day, Iris was working on her project. She was happy that she could focus, think, and generate new approaches to accomplish her daily work. As soon as she finished her work, she now needed to make a few phone calls and send a few e-mails. She felt that she needed to be in a nice, kind, and caring mode. Then, it was almost three in the afternoon. She was trying to change her mental and spiritual mode to be lovely and smiley for her husband and kids. Then, it was the prayer

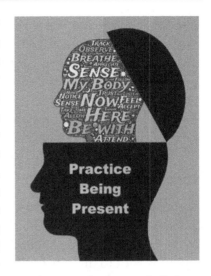

and chanting time. She started praying. She was thinking of all these modes of changing personalities and their difficulties. Then, she said to herself, "It is possible, but not easy."

IN PRACTICE

It is important to be fully in the space and time. Due to changing venues, sometimes one can have spiritual and social accidents. In these accidents, people can find the person rude, harsh, and not caring. It is important to accept the difficulty of changing personalities while changing venues and time. One of the ways to make it easy is to establish constant prayers and chants during the day. This can help person to focus, self-reflect, detach, and discharge spiritual toxicity.

Discussion Question

► Can a person only assume one personality? Why?

16. Little Minds Thinking Big

One day, Sophia went with her four-year-old to a science museum. There were skeletons of dinosaurs and other fossils. Her four-year-old son was amazed and asked questions constantly. Sophia was surprised about the quality of the questions from a four-year-old. She said to herself, "Wow, a person can start the journey even if they are only four years old. The important part is how to gauge and help them."

IN PRACTICE

It is important to realize that sometimes little minds can really think big. In this process of imagination, if they are not engaged correctly, after years of childhood and adulthood, these memories and conversations can come back to the person. These memories can sometimes be fake, illusion, or it can be something positive in one's relationship with God. In other words, the personal religious experience can start from early childhood years with understanding nature, art, and sounds. On the other hand, there are some scholars who try to limit the kids' exposure to visual and audio related items such as pictures or music. Their reasoning is that a child may not know how to transform those meanings from these visual and audio sources into meanings. Therefore, these sources can become isolating in their construction of a positive relationship with the Divine.

Discussion Question

► How do you relate your childhood religious experience to your current religious practice?

17. Anger and Difficulty

A month passed. Mia was so nice to her kids. She has not been angry. One day, the kids as usual did something annoying and not respectful to their mom. She burst out with anger towards them. Then, after a while, she calmed down. She said to herself, "I was doing fine for some time and didn't get angry but controlled my anger. What happened to me? I lost myself again." She went back to her kids and discussed the reason why she got angry, gave advice to them, and also asked forgiveness from them.

IN PRACTICE

It is good to give advice. How to give the advice can be more important than the content of the advice. In other words, it is very challenging to give advice without being angry but genuinely relating the message in a way that others do not get offended. This communication and attitude can become more challenging with the people that we see every day at work or at home. It is also important to regret how we talk or feel about others. Therefore, it is a virtue to say one is sorry and ask forgiveness from the people if there is any possibility of breaking their hearts.

Discussion Question

► Do you practice self-reflection often?

18. Trials, Position of the Heart, and Detachment

One day, Ella was thinking about the wisdom behind trials, hardships, and difficulties. Then, she met a friend who was living a very rich and nice life but was not attached to her possessions. Later, she met another friend who was poor, sick, and always fearful of becoming even poorer and losing what she had. Then, Ella looked at the two cases and said to herself, "I found it. It is detachment from what you have."

IN PRACTICE

A person can be rich or poor, having an easy life or difficult life. It is not important. The important part is the position of the heart, if changing, as a sign of attachment to them. If a person's heart is the same in the happiest times of his or her life, and the same in the most difficult times of his or her life, then this person is detached from everything except the fulfilment of the choice of God. If it becomes a constant trait of a person, then it becomes a spiritual station. Then, this is the real joy, happiness, and heaven for the person in the world.

19. Heart Diseases and Detection

One day, Chloe was praying in a park. Her kids were playing. There was another family and a small girl. Chloe gave one candy to all of her children. Her kids came and asked her for seconds and she said, "No." Then, a small girl came to Chloe and asked for a candy. She gave her a candy. Then, after the girl finished her candy, she came and asked for another one. Chloe was thinking, "What should I say? I have a few more candies left. They are expensive". Chloe told the small girl to wait. She was looking in her bag to see if she can give something else to the small girl. Realizing this, the small girl's mother came and got very angry at the small girl. She felt horrible and said, "My stinginess!"

IN PRACTICE

Like the above story, Chloe immediately tried to detect her spiritual disease in the incident instead of blaming the mother. In spiritual endeavors, it is a level to know one's own spiritual disease. Then, one can work on his or her disease. Stinginess is a disease that sometimes may be hard to detect. Stinginess is a sign of attachment which can be the opposite of the positive spiritual state of detachment. Every positive spiritual state can be the opposite of a spiritual disease.

Discussion Question

▶   Is it difficult to detect one's own spiritual diseases? Why?

20. Having Egyptian Coffee

One day, James was in a coffee shop in Cairo. He enjoyed different types of coffee in Egypt. While he was drinking coffee, he was chatting with the store owner. The owner mentioned that the Elite Egyptians prefer Starbucks over local coffee. James said, "I don't know why people always want what they don't have."

IN PRACTICE

The positive attitude of what one already has, is the first step of gratitude and thankfulness to God. In this sense, positive local or hometown support for the ownership of a business market can be similar to someone having what one has in the spiritual journey with the attitude of gratefulness and thankfulness.

21. Thirsty Child

One day, Lila was traveling with her child in the car. Her child got thirsty. Then, he asked his mom, "May I have some water?" His mom said, "Okay, when we stop at a gas station, then we will get a bottle for you." The kid was very thirsty. He kept asking every other minute. His mom kept saying, "Okay, I will get it soon." The kid said, "Sorry, I forgot that I asked before." A minute later the kid came back with the same question. The mom said to herself, "I should stop immediately, or he will keep asking."

IN PRACTICE

When a person is thirsty, the need for finding water becomes so urgent for him or her. This urge can make the person want to get water as soon as possible. Similarly, if the person does not need to have a spiritual path, he or she cannot benefit from great teachers or from great experiential sessions of meditation, prayers, and retreats.

22. Checking the Heart

One day, Riley visited a poor city in Cairo. She was staying in a nice, expensive hotel. She went outside to take a walk. There were a lot of beggars coming and asking money from her. Riley tried to always keep some money for the poor in her pocket. As she was giving the money to one beggar, other beggars came and asked for more money from her. Riley said her money was finished. The beggar insisted and Riley felt uncomfortable. For a minute she made self-reflection on her heart to check if there were any judgment feelings towards the beggar. She said, "But it was not easy."

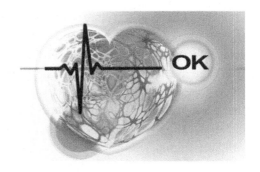

IN PRACTICE

It is important to check one's heart constantly. Any type of arrogance, judgment of others, feelings of superiority, disgust, or ridicule are some examples of dangerous cases for the heart. In the above case, Riley tried to help people without judgment, but with empathy for their situations. In the case of one beggar insisting on more money, she tried to neutralize her heart in order to not have any type of bad feelings towards the beggar. The real state of the heart can be with detachment from worldly endeavors although Riley stayed in an expensive hotel. It is not the physical or external detachment, but detachment of the heart from everything except God.

Discussion Question

► How one can make the habit of checking their hearts? Is this difficult?

23. Funeral and Crying

One day, Mason came to his home. He heard his wife crying in the other room and talking on the phone. As soon as Mason overheard the word 'funeral', he understood what was going on. Without going to the room next to his wife, Mason sat and engaged himself with his regular daily routine of meditation and prayer. Then, his wife came from the other room and told the news about their loss. Mason said, "We belong to God and will return back to God."

IN PRACTICE

It is important to have a daily routine of meditation, prayer, and reflection time. This becomes more critical when someone is hit with an evil-seeming incident. At these times, this routine practice of the person allows the person to collect oneself spiritually and keep the spiritual composure and calmness. In the above story, instead of rushing to his wife about the loss, Mason first rushed to God for self-spiritual strength to help others. After becoming empowered with his daily routine practice of meditation, prayer, and reflection, he then helped his wife.

24. Chats Leading to Disturbance

One day, Logan was chatting with his mother. As he did not like to talk too much so as not to make mistakes and displease God, he said to himself, "This is my old mother. Let me chat a little bit to entertain her." Logan started chatting with a normal conversation similar to others. They were talking about weather, food, kids, and people. He became a little bit uneasy while the topic was about people. He was trying not to backbite or talk bad about others. As the conversation continued, Logan said something about a person that disturbed him so much and he said to himself, "I wish I did not talk and as usual observed silence instead."

IN PRACTICE

Silence, smiling, and greeting people are some of the encouraged ways by the prophets. It is expected that if a person talks, then they should have a reason. Any talk or conversation without purpose can lead to uneasy states of heart due to sins such as backbiting of others, showing signs of arrogance, etc. It is very difficult to balance the two modes of social life compared to introvert life with oneself. The prophets showed a good model of this balance. They used to always smile and greet people. Everyone was very comfortable around them. On the other hand, when they talked it had a purpose. Their speech was very concise, to the point, and at the same time, dense in various meanings. There are a lot of narrations stating that people could have counted the number of words that he used while he was talking.

25. Hugging, Anger, and Child

One day, a father got angry with his kids. The youngest went to him and started hugging and kissing his dad. He then started kissing and hugging him, too. He then said to himself, "I was angry, but I am not anymore. What happened to me?"

IN PRACTICE

It is important to be insistent and demanding in asking forgiveness from God. The prophets mention that when a person prays and asks for forgiveness from God, he or she should be firm and insistent. God can do anything. There is no human association of anger for God in practice. Anger is something negative and a defect in human discourses. Instead, one can use the phrase 'God's displeasure'.

26. Controlling the Heart and Thoughts

One day, Luke met a person who was mean to others about their faults and was not respectful in religious matters. A year passed and Luke was invited to a social gathering. He was not sure if he should go or not. He did not have a clear intention for why he would want to participate in the gathering. Then, he decided to attend and happened to meet the same mean and disrespectful person in this social gathering. The person was paralyzed. Luke felt bad for him and tried to stop his thoughts and disposition of his heart about the possible reasons for this person's difficulty.

IN PRACTICE

It is important to make intention as to why to do something or not. Mere intention of having fun or no intention can put the person in jeopardy regarding one's relationship with God in case something happens. In the above story, when Luke attended the gathering and saw the person who used to be mean and disrespectful, his immediate and uncontrolled urge was to relate what happened to him with his prior improper disposition with people and religion. Now, Luke put himself in a difficult self-control position fighting against and stopping these thoughts coming to his mind and heart. In practice, a person does not judge others, especially with their difficulties. There are a lot of incidents wherein if people judge others, the same problems and issues can occur with them.

27. The Lonely Wise-Fool

There was a lonely wise-fool who used to come to the temple. Everyone used to make a joke of him. He did not show up for a few weeks in the temple. Then, one day in very cold weather, he came to the temple. He did not properly dress to protect himself from the freezing cold weather. While he was leaving, the people advised him not to go out without any gloves or jacket because he may get sick and even die. The wise-fool got very angry and said, "I have been in my home for a long time and no one asks about me. Why do you care about me now?"

IN PRACTICE

It is important to check on people as we are all humans. People get lonely, depressed, and need company. A simple phone call, or a quick visit can prevent terrific spiritual depressions and dead ends.

28. Being with Old Friends, the Journey, and Progress

One day, Zoe went to visit her old friends. She was enjoying her time as they were talking about some religious topics on the journey. Zoe realized that her old friends are still at the same spiritual level. When she gave her disposition about the topic discussed, her friends realized that Zoe had gone so far and was at a much higher level. Then, Zoe realized this and said, "This could be a trap!"

IN PRACTICE

It is important to desire progress on the spiritual journey in one's relationship with God. Everyone has a different pace on the journey. Some may not make much progress but preserve what they have. Some will go back. Some will stay with not much progress. Some will excel much in the race of the journey. It is very critical to increase the self-reflection, repentance, gratitude, and humility for God. If not, the progress itself can have some black holes like traps to suck the person in, that the person may not realize. Some of these black but invisible holes can be the feelings of arrogance, superiority, and vanity. In this perspective, in the above story, when Zoe realized this, she immediately asked for forgiveness and made repentance to God.

29. The Divorce

One day, Dylan was upset with his kids and family. He woke up in the morning and said to himself, "It is the weekend. Everyone is home. I should not be angry." He then decided to leave home and go to the temple to pray for spiritual strength and help from God. The temple was empty except for a man that Dylan had not seen before. The man was praying as well. After completing the prayer, Dylan had a chat with the man. The man said, "I am going through a divorce. Please pray for me." The man was married for 22 years and he had seven children. Dylan tried to counsel the man if there was a way to save the marriage. The man said, "I want to get out of it and be with God. Before I die, I want to do what I want to do. I am 55 years old." He said, "Okay, can you be a shadow man at home and keep the marriage and still spend your time in worship of God?" The man insisted that it was not possible. Dylan said to himself, "God sent me a person to help me to be patient in my problems."

IN PRACTICE

It is always encouraged to run to God in times of difficulty and uneasiness. Both the man and Dylan ran to the temple to pray and ask for help. Dylan took a lesson for himself from the man's situation because this man was going through divorce. It is important to prevent something disliked like divorce if it is possible. If it is not possible, by all means, then God allows the divorce, but it should be the last resort, not the first one. It is important to realize that one can worship and spend time with God while still having social and family engagements, although it may be sometimes difficult. Therefore, it is ideal to keep both but not sacrifice one or another if possible.

30. The Bad News Giver: Did You Know What Happened?

One day, Levi saw a man in the temple. For Levi, this man's title was 'Bad News Giver'. Each time Levi saw him, he would give tragic news by stating, "Did you know what happened?" Then, he would report, for example, "There was an accident on the highway. People died." Or, "There is a snowstorm coming tonight. There is a traffic ban," and other news. Each time Levi heard about it, he used to not be disturbed, but would focus on his prayers, chants, and meditation.

IN PRACTICE

It is important to prepare oneself for the outcomes of one's life journey. One day, a person came to the prophets and asked, "When is the end of the world and accountability in front of God?" The prophets replied to him and said, "What did you prepare for it?" It is more important to have a schedule in one's relationship with God rather than elaborating on the unseen or unexpected events called 'news'. Therefore, a person who is at a spiritual level of neutrality, is not very affected by the news of evil-seeming or good-seeming incidents.

31. Cooking and Talking

One day, Isaac attended a spiritual gathering. There was a person hard pressed in life suffering some hardships at this gathering. The topic of conversation was the concept of destiny and one's relationship with God. Although Isaac was holding himself in so as not to talk and to be in silent mode, there was some misunderstanding about the concept of theodicy, so he felt that he needed to express his stance and he explained the ideal expected disposition of a person in these discussions. After he left this gathering, he felt uneasy. He said to himself, "I hope I did not imply anything that would make that hard-pressed person feel guilty and worse. I wish I didn't talk as I promised myself before that I wouldn't."

IN PRACTICE

It is really difficult to keep the balance of talking and silence. When a person talks, it is expected that the person ponders well before putting thoughts into words. In this case, using a language and voice tone without irritating others is similar to heat, fire, or an oven. Having empathy for others is the spice of speech. However, the main ingredient of talking is addressing one's own self or ego in order to better it, but not to better the other person. In this regard, Isaac had a hard time balancing all of these critical elements as mentioned in the above story.

32. Intention and Difficulties

One day, Mateo attended a difficult religious gathering. He forgot to make his intention before attending. During this gathering, people were discussing religious matters in impolite etiquette. Mateo tried to contribute with his 'two cents' but was not sure if it would be useful. He did not feel well as usual and left. He said to himself, "Why did I come here?"

IN PRACTICE

It is important to make your intention before you do anything. Sometimes, things may look straightforward, but even in these times, it is important to renew and repeat one's intention to get the highest benefit. Sometimes, the person may be in unpleasant situations that one may not expect. If the person had a good intention in these cases, then still, the person is rewarded by God due to one's intention. In the above story, Mateo had a problem with himself in that he forgot to make an intention for attendance of the gathering. When he encountered a difficult and unpleasant environment, he went back to his intention to seek comfort and relief, but he realized that he did not make an intention before his action.

33. People's Sensitivity and Culture

Charles did not like to talk to people in the mornings. When he used to go to temple, he used to prefer silence. A man from a different culture came one morning to Charles to visit him in the temple. This man loved Charles very much. He was upset, too. He said to him, "What did I do to you? Why are you not talking to me?" Charles handed him some coffee and wrote on a paper that he loves him too, but he is busy now and he cannot talk. The man was still upset but kept talking to Charles and complaining about his silent treatment. Charles kept the silence, put his head down, and listened to the man. Afterwards, the man left and Charles said to himself, "I should be more sensitive of different cultures. Not everyone understands what I am doing."

IN PRACTICE

Silence is the default mode of a person who is not talking. Especially, there are ones who are on the path who prefer to be silent at different times of the day such as mornings until they finish their daily dialogue with God. At these times, the person wants to focus on their relationship with God without any external, even internal, disturbances of thoughts or feelings. When people are engaged at these times, some cannot fully pay attention to the etiquettes of social interactions. An outsider should always maintain good thoughts about others, in this case about Charles in the above story. Yet, at the same time, Charles should try to recognize the cultural and social sensitivities of people to prevent more evil that may lead to more disturbing headaches later.

34. The Best Voice

There was a man in the mosque who thought he had the best voice when he used to sing to call people to prayer. As soon as he would sing the prayer call, the people in the mosque would leave in order to not hear his voice until he was done. They waited outside and then came back. He actually had a very bad voice. One day, this man came into the mosque and brought the recording of a famous prayer singer and said, "Can you please listen to this famous singer and tell me who sings the prayer call better? Me or him?"

IN PRACTICE

Sometimes, the spiritual diseases can become the character of a person if there is no fellow friend telling the person of his or her mistakes. Therefore, it is a practice to have friends, not wives or husbands, to tell you your mistakes rather than simply praising your achievements. One scholar says, "I love a friend who warns me about a scorpion on my chest. Why should I get angry with her?"

35. The Door and the Responsibility

Everyone was coming to listen to the Friday sermon in the temple. Adam was in the temple as well. He was sitting next to the outside door. The famous assistant priest of the temple was sitting next to Adam. As people were coming inside, they were closing the door and locking it by mistake. Each time, the priest was getting up and unlocking the door and telling the people to leave the door open. Another man came in and did the same as the others, closing the door which would then lock itself. Another, another, another . . . The poor priest was getting annoyed and getting up and sitting down. Adam was watching and smiling . . .

IN PRACTICE

Similarly, there are people who work in the churches, temples, or mosques. They may be externally close to worshipping God, but they are actually very distracted and very far away from God. Sometimes the closeness can make the person blind. It can have an opposite effect. A person looking to the brightness of the sun can become blind. Satan was very close to God but lost. Similarly, some religious people believe that God is so obvious that if people cannot see God then it is because of the blindness due to the clear brightness.

36. Coffee Machine and Generosity

There was a poor man in a temple. He bought a small coffee machine for a dollar and he put it in the temple. While he was staying in the temple, he was drinking coffee by himself. If people came to the temple, he used to give the leftover coffee to them. As time passed, people started respecting him because he was giving coffee to everyone. One day, a person brought some cookies and put them next to the coffee on the serving table. The following day, a person brought crackers. Every day now there were some drinks and food in the temple.

IN PRACTICE

The best way of teaching in practice is being an example rather than preaching to people. The starter of a good action receives from God each individual's rewards as well.

37. Gavin and People's Jealousy

As Gavin was spending most of his time in the temple, everyone was getting annoyed with him. People were gossiping and saying, "We are working, and this guy is spending all his time here, worshipping." His wife was getting annoyed with him as well because he was spending all of his time with worship and she was complaining to him that she always wanted to worship like him but she was not able to do it. Gavin realized this and said to himself, "What should I do before these people destroy me with their jealousy? I need to hide myself . . ."

IN PRACTICE

It is a very common historical occurrence that jealousy of people always puts religious people in jeopardy. Therefore, some try to pretend to be insane. Some leave people altogether and live in the mountains or in caves. Some try to pretend or take the title of being the cleaner of a temple or a temple.

38. The Sunglasses

There were two people in the temple. One was rich but used to buy cheap clothes. The other was poor but always wanted to buy expensive clothes. One day, the rich man went to a dollar store to buy sunglasses. Then, he went to the temple with his new sunglasses. The poor man saw him with his new sunglasses and said: "You look very nice with your expensive sunglasses." The rich man smiled and took the sunglasses and gave them to the poor man as a gift. The poor man was so happy.

IN PRACTICE

Sometimes, on the spiritual path, a person can assume and put a value on something that is invaluable for God. The external can be deceptive when one assesses its real value. The people's attachment to the world, wealth, and luxury are examples of these incorrect assessments.

39. On the Beaches of Miami

There were two friends. One, Kevin, was a regular temple attendee, spending most of his time in the temple, and enjoying the prayers and reading the scriptures. The other, Rowan, was spending most of his time on the beaches of Miami, enjoying the sun, and while enjoying, performing his prayers and readings from the scripture. One day, Kevin wanted to visit Rowan. He was worried about his friend's spirituality because he was spending most of his time on the beach. Kevin took a plane and went to Miami and found his friend on the beach. Kevin was very uncomfortable because the beach was not like the temple. He was walking and looking down and trying to find his friend and not be affected by the naked scenes of the opposite gender. Finally, he found his friend and immediately asked the question, "I really don't understand. How can you pray and read your scripture here?" Rowan said, "They are not attractive. I don't look at them."

IN PRACTICE

In normative teachings, an unwanted look, sight, or hearing can affect the heart of the person. There may be some exceptions to the general rule depending on the special circumstance of the person, similar to the story mentioned above.

40. The One Who Talks a Lot When He Is at Fault

One day Ryder was late to the class. The teacher was angry but did not show his anger. Ryder immediately engaged with the class discussion to pretend that he had been there since the beginning of the class. The other students understood this and were annoyed.

IN PRACTICE

Sometimes, the faults can paint the mind and the heart as a result of not accepting one's mistakes. A person on the path is expected to face all mistakes during the course of the day. It should be the accountability of all actions, words, sentences, sounds, sights, and tastes. At the end of the day, the person can self-evaluate all of his or her dealings and whether they were necessary or not. Then, the next day, the person can become more careful. At least he or she can eliminate some of them in the beginning of this new day. For some scholars, one's realization of his or her mistakes is also a positive achievement on the spiritual path. One of the worst levels of the spiritual path is not realizing one's mistakes or not being aware of them.

41. Backbiting and Arguing

Max was sitting in the temple. Some people were talking and laughing about the ugliness of a girl. Max heard this and was disgusted about their enjoyment of their backbiting, eating the flesh of their sister. When Max heard this conversation, he stepped away from them in order to not listen to them. Next morning, Max entered the temple. He saw the same people who were laughing, but now were arguing with each other and they were so angry with each other.

IN PRACTICE

The effect of something evil can manifest itself as another disturbance. The people talked badly about a poor girl and enjoyed it and now they are fighting with each other over some nonsense.

42. Silence

One day Ivy attended a religious retreat for self-discipline. She saw a friend of hers that she had not seen for a long time. Her friend asked how Ivy was doing all of these years. Ivy started explaining in detail what had transpired in all of those past years.

Finally, it was Ivy's turn to ask the same question of her friend and she said, "So, how have you been? What did you do all of these years that I didn't see you?" Her friend replied, "I am sorry. I cannot talk because the teacher in the self-discipline retreat said that you can eat but you can't talk." Ivy was so annoyed.

IN PRACTICE

There are three main principles on the spiritual path—minimizing talking, eating, and sleeping. In the above story, the teacher in the retreat let the new practitioners eat whatever they wanted but tried to discipline talking only as a method of teaching. In practice it is understood that the amount of talking, eating, and sleeping are all related. In this case of self-discipline training, the teacher focused only on habitual talking. Ivy was annoyed because her friend let her talk without telling her of the teacher's recommendation at the beginning of their conversation. If Ivy knew this, she wouldn't have engaged in talking and wouldn't have told her friend in detail about her life.

43. Julia and the Professor

One day Julia was giving a lecture on the concept of understanding submission, reliance, and surrender in relationship with God. There was a professor who was sitting as a student in the class. The professor did not get what Julia was trying to say. A few years later, Julia received a phone call from the professor. The professor was crying and said, "I understand what you meant by surrender now. My wife had cancer. I was distraught. She was getting worse in front of me every day in the hospital. I could not help her. I thought that I was powerful and confident. She died. I submit and surrender."

IN PRACTICE

It is very important to embody the notion that all of a person's physical and spiritual power is from God. In other words, the person should believe and embody that one cannot even lift his or her arm or be in a good spiritual engagement unless there is a blessing and opening from God. There are phrases that people chant daily to instill this notion for the spiritual traveler. In the above story, the professor trusted and relied on his own power in his dealings with life and he suffered.

44. Bad Word

There were two kids who were memorizing the Scriptures. They were playing in the temple and Kaiden was busy with his reflection. One of the kids said a bad word to another one. Kaiden called the boys and said, "Make a choice. Good words and bad words do not stay at the same time in the heart." A good word and a bad word cannot occupy the same place in one's heart at the same time. If you say a bad word, all the good words and your memorization will leave you.

IN PRACTICE

A person's intake of good food, good words, or good smells makes a good spiritual heart. One of the best good words is the word of God. The Scriptures are pure and clean. Therefore, a person cannot touch the Scriptures before washing oneself. A person will not be able to memorize something purely if his or her tongue and mind are engaged with anger, backbiting, jealousy, and anything that does not concern the person. This notion is much embedded in the advice of the prophets for the ones who want to memorize the Scriptures.

45. Shouting

There were two people arguing and shouting in the temple. Calvin was in the temple, too. As soon as Calvin heard their shouting, he left the temple.

IN PRACTICE

When there is shouting among people, then that environment is contaminated with bad spirits instead of the angelic beings. Actually, there are verses in the Scriptures [31:19] that discourage shouting as a way of communication. Bad spirits encourage bad words, shouting, anger, and physical harm. Angelic beings, the Scriptures, the chanting, and prayer inspire good words and peaceful feelings and tranquility.

46. The Man with One Leg and The Man with One Eye

One day Vivian was talking with her nephew on the phone. Her nephew lost most of his sight in one of his eyes. This was due to a tumor behind his eyes. Her nephew was upset. He used to be a good-looking man. While talking with her nephew, Vivian saw a man with one leg using crutches and going to the temple to pray. She inquired of her nephew:

> Vivian: Do you prefer to have two eyes—one perfect and the other not seeing well—or do you prefer to have two perfect eyes, but only one leg?

> Nephew: It is tough. I prefer what I have now because I do not know if what you describe is more complicated or painful for me.

IN PRACTICE

Appreciation without any complaints in relationship with God is the key. The phrase 'thank you God' represents this notion of appreciation in the relationship with the Divine in all circumstances. In the above story, the one-legged man was struggling to go to the temple to pray to God in order to appreciate what he has. Sometimes, people look at what they do not have and complain instead of appreciating what they do have and being thankful in their relationship with God.

47. The Right Answer

Camden was in the temple. A man with inflexible beliefs came and wanted to do some missionary work. He wanted Camden to go with him. Camden did not want to go but he said to himself, "If I say that I don't want to go, he will argue with me and I don't want to waste my time." He said to the man "I will think about it . . ." The man left him alone.

IN PRACTICE

It is always important to reflect and think well before uttering any words to any person. Therefore, religious people prefer silence and purposeful talking if and when necessary. If they are put in a difficult situation of choice, they try to use wisdom to minimize any evil and undesired effects.

48. Not Flying

There was a man who went to the airport to take his brother who was flying to England. As his brother was going to the plane, he waved to his brother and said to himself, "I will never fly to England. It is such an ugly country." After a few years, he went to England and he liked it so much. He said to himself, "I should not have had those thoughts in my mind."

IN PRACTICE

In the above history, he did not want to fly to England and had some negative thoughts about it. God made him fly there in order to rectify his thoughts about different places and people.

49. Change and God

One day Ava saw her old friend with another person that she had not seen for a few years. After the greetings, her old friend started introducing her. Ava was a little bit uncomfortable because William was not the same William that her friend used to know a few years ago. Every hour he was different.

IN PRACTICE

In genuine practice, change and advancement on the spiritual path is good. Every day a person is expected to go further in the closeness and union with God. The only unchanged One is God. God's attributes are constant and unchanged—the difference between the creation and Creator.

50. Liam and the Handyman

Liam was with a drunk, poor handyman. Liam was trying to help him by giving him some work at his house and advising him on changing his bad and destructive habits. The handyman was coming to the Liam's home. One day, Liam gave him a small loan so that the handyman could buy a car and not be dependent on people, because with gambling and drinking he had lost everything. Then, Liam saw a dream the same night that the handyman's face was turned into a fox and was snickering and smiling. Liam woke up and didn't understand what the dream meant. Then, he called the handyman, but he didn't answer. One call, two, three, many calls, no answer . . . Next day, next month, no answer from the handyman. Liam was worried about the handyman. He said to himself, "I hope he is OK. I don't care about the loan." Then, finally, he reached one of his friends. His friend said he left town and will not come back again. Liam said, "Thank God, he is OK."

IN PRACTICE

In genuine practice, thinking good about people is the key even though the people may have bad traits. In the above story, it seems that the handyman intended to leave the town without paying Liam. Therefore, he seemed to trick Liam as shown within his dream interpretation. Although Liam might have understood the meaning of his dream, still he was worried about the handyman, not his money.

51. The Teacher and the Kids

There was a teacher in the mosque who used to teach the kids. After shouting at the kids, he used to give candies. Although the teacher seemed to be angry and shouting to an outsider, the kids seemed to love him. He used to smile also and explain the lecture well. Kids seemed to interpret the teacher's treatment not as abuse or hate, but as a method of teaching. The kids felt this genuine intention and feelings from the teacher. Fatima was watching this and said to herself, "Wow, this is similar to the relationship between the person and God."

IN PRACTICE

God does not get angry like humans. Anger in humans can be a deficient quality. God gives opportunities and learning experiences to people to excel in the path of perfecting their relationship with the Divine. It is up to the person to take heed from each experience as a self-learning opportunity to build a positive relationship with God.

52. Rotation of the Days

Ali in the temple. An old man came and said that his car was stolen. Ali was trying to help the person to call the police. He felt bad for the old man. Then, Ali went to his home. His wife said that her best friend's sister is dying due to pancreatic cancer. Ali was sad and prayed for her. Then, he got sick and was admitted to the emergency room. Ali thought about all these recent incidents and smiled to himself, "Rotation of the days."

IN PRACTICE

In spiritualism, God rotates evil-looking or good-looking days among people to reveal the real character of the people. Below is a passage from the scriptures that alludes to this notion.

If an evil touch you
Then remember that
Evil touches others as well.

These are the days
We rotate among the people
Good and evil

So that the real characters
Of people are revealed
God knows it and
You become witness to it as well

Remember God does not like oppressors.

One of the states in practice is the station of patience. When evil hits the person, if the person does not complain but still appreciates what comes from God, then the person can use this as an opportunity to excel spiritually. In practice, everyone asks for goodness and an easy life. If for some reason it does not happen, the notion of patience is practiced. In both good-looking and evil-looking days, the person appreciates the relationship with God.

53. Temporary Things

One day, Mason missed his wife very much. He went home to see her but did not receive much attention from her. Then, he left his home. Next day, he missed his daughter and went home to see her. His daughter did not care that he came home, and Mason was disappointed. Then, he left his home. Next day, he missed his friends that he used to hang around. He went to visit his friends. His friends were in their own world and Mason felt disconnected from them. Then, he left them. Finally, he decided to visit the places where he was born and where he had spent all of his childhood years. He went there and found that everything looked different and he felt so isolated and deeply in pain. At the end, he understood that he needs to travel to the internal house.

IN PRACTICE

In religious writings, the house generally symbolizes the heart where the person has a close relationship with God. In the above story, Mason was disappointed with the temporary friends. At the end, he turned to the permanent, real, appreciative, and understanding Friend—God. In practice, it is believed that everything can be a cause of pain except God. Everything can include all of one's loved ones, friends, and family members. A person among loved ones can be lonely. A person in prison can be happy, enjoying all pleasures.

54. The Uber Driver, Cursing, and the Coffee

As Samantha was late to her appointment, she called Uber to get there instead of taking the bus. A nice Uber car came and picked her up. The driver was so nice and Samantha was enjoying the ride. Then, there was a car which abruptly cut off the road in front of this Uber car. The Uber driver started cursing the other car and he became so disturbed. Samantha was watching the scene and trying to get a meaning from it. They finally reached their destination. While Samantha was leaving the car, she forgot her coffee in the car. The driver called her and said, "You forgot your coffee. That is the most important thing." Samantha smiled and then said to herself, "This is the reason why the driver was so disturbed. There is no Union."

IN PRACTICE

A person's real spiritual state can reveal itself at the encounters of different evil-looking incidents. In the above story, although the driver seemed very nice in the beginning, he lost his temper in a very small evil-looking incident. When he mentioned that "the coffee is the most important thing," then Samantha interpreted that the driver's short temperament is due to his engagement with temporal things such as coffee. A person in practice gets real empowerment from the permanent One, God, on the journey.

55. The Crying Boy

Alex saw a father and a son. The boy was crying for something futile. The father was looking at him and he was feeling bad for his son. The father did not give what the boy wanted. The boy was still crying and trying to get the attention of the father. At the end, the father taught a lesson to his son and gave him better than what he wanted, and the son was so happy. Alex was looking at the scene and said, "That is the relation between God and a person."

IN PRACTICE

In religious practice, a person prays constantly, cries, and asks. It may be that the person is asking for something futile, useless, or harmful. During the time of asking and crying through prayer, the person can feel pain and neglected. Sometimes, they may even think, "Why are my prayers not being accepted?" The One, who is always Active, Hearing, and Merciful appreciates the effort and sincere humbleness of the person in relationship with the Creator. At the end, due to these efforts, God can give the person better than what is asked for, although the person may not initially understand this.

56. The Huffing and Puffing Man

There was a man who used to come to the temple and pray. He used to constantly come and tell his problems to Cameron. This man used to complain about his family members and other people, claiming that everyone was always unjust to him. If Cameron wanted to give him some advice, he did not want to listen—only talk and blame others. One day, Cameron was in the temple studying. This man came and he was huffing and puffing. He saw Cameron studying and did not want to disturb him. Cameron understood the case and prolonged his studying in order to not be disturbed. The man was pacing back and forth in the temple, huffing and puffing, waiting and peering in on Cameron to find out if he finished his studying so that he could talk to him as usual. Five minutes, ten minutes, half an hour, one hour . . . Cameron was still studying. His head was in the book and the man was circulating within the temple, huffing and puffing and checking to see if Cameron had finished his studying. Cameron smiled and said to himself, "I know you want to talk to me, but I know I can't help you until you sit down and engage yourself with reading the scripture, engage in prayer and chanting, and do some self-reflection. Then your problems will be solved."

IN PRACTICE

Humans really don't solve any problems. Even their apathy and lack of concern about one's problem can add more pain to the person's suffering. The real helper, listener, and concerned is only One, God. Although the person may think that no one is hearing or talking back, the mystical answers from God can be revealed to the person whether the person understands or not.

57. The Cat and the Natural Habitat

One day Caroline visited a friend of hers in America. Her friend had an indoor cat. Caroline was surprised that the cats were kept at home and they were not allowed to go outside. Each morning when Caroline woke up, she saw that the cats were rushing to the window to look outside as her friend was opening the blinds. One day, Caroline said to her friend, "Can I please take them into the backyard for a few minutes? I feel that it is their natural habitat. I feel bad for them as they rush every morning to look out the window." Her friend said, "Okay." Caroline opened the glass door from the house to the backyard. The cats came to the edge of the door and they were scared to go outside, and they didn't go. Caroline was thinking . . . and finally she smiled and said, "This is exactly the relationship between the person and God. The cats need time."

IN PRACTICE

In religions, it is the human's genuine nature to establish a relationship with God. In a pure human self, a person can feel this desire and needs it fully. As the person grows, if the person moves away from his or her pure self, an artificial, trained self can replace that in the person. Then, abnormal can become normal. Unnatural can become natural. In the above story, since the cats were domesticated to stay at home, they felt that something was pulling them to their natural habitat. Therefore, they rushed every day to observe the sun, plants, and other beings from the window of the house. In this new self of the cats, when they were invited to go to their natural habitat they were scared. Caroline said, "The cats need time" to indicate that to transform from unnatural to natural, it can take time, but it is possible. One can always re-establish a natural relationship with one's own pure self and God, but it can require time, sincere effort, and good teachers.

58. Men and Women

Jason was often upset that his wife was not spending much time with him as they grew older in their marriage. He was thinking about this. As he was reflecting on the marital problems of others, he realized that he had some similar problems. One night, he was disturbed by this and woke up in the middle of the night and prayed in order to receive some guidance from God. At the end, he said, "I got it. Men can become more sensitive as they grow older and expect more attention like a child. As men get older, they don't feel that they have enough attention from their wives. Then, they can make a problem and even get divorced with different types of blame. Women can be more independent and still maintain the rationality compared to men. Therefore, I see a lot of men being taken care of by their wives in their old age. I think this is the root of my problem. God knows best."

IN PRACTICE

It is important to correctly detect one's own problems and disturbances through self-reflection and focus. In a religion, there is a lot of advice recommending to solve problems at night while people are sleeping through prayers and invocation to God. In the above story, Jason got guidance to rationalize the source of his problem. Therefore, he can now discipline his own perception in his marital relationship.

59. "Staying Out of Trouble"

There was a man who used to come to the temple. He was very friendly and always seemed very happy. Each time Logan saw this man, he used to say, "I am trying to stay out of trouble." Logan used to smile and think about what he meant. One year passed, two years . . . and more. Each time Logan saw this man, he would say, "I am trying to stay out of trouble." One day, Logan had a car accident. He smiled and understood why the man kept repeating this phrase. Logan said to himself, "Having a day without any problem is a blessing and requires gratitude to God."

IN PRACTICE

Sometimes, a person may expect extraordinary things in life in order to be thankful to God on the journey. One can understand the value and happiness of the previous day when experiencing a difficulty or a problem in the present day. Therefore, a day without any evil or problem can elicit thankfulness and gratitude to God.

60. The Floating Wood Log on the Sea

There was a physicist called Nolan walking on the seashore with his friend. While enjoying their walk, they saw a wood log on the sea, floating nicely on the sea's surface. The physicist Nolan asked his friend, "Why do you think this log does not sink?" His friend thought Nolan expected an answer from physics because he was a physicist and continued explaining all the laws of physics. Then, Nolan the physicist said, "Actually, the wood log does not sink because it does not panic." His friend smiled…

IN PRACTICE

There are always external and internal meanings to every minute detail of life. In the above story, although the wood log was very heavy, it did not sink and was nicely floating. Nolan imagined a person's reasons, reactions, reasoning, feelings, and thoughts when they encounter something fearful and stressful and get trapped in it and die. One can consider a person who can die while swimming if there is panic or stress. Similarly, in spiritual endeavors, knowledge and practice help the person to not die in fear-provoking or evil-looking incidents. Actually, the person can enjoy this situation if the person knows how to submit and surrender instead of suffering and dying from it, similar to the case of the floating wood log in the story above. This spiritual level may take time, and practice, and one may need knowledge. It may not be easy to adopt it in the beginning of the journey.

61. Final Stage of the Fireworks

Angle was a giving a lecture. One of the students, who was in his seventies, asked a question. He revealed that he was having more spiritual experiences as he grew older and he asked the reason for this. Angle smiled and said, "In the fireworks show, there are more extensive displays as it approaches the end. Similarly, every journey has an end. As it gets close to the end, the signs may increase."

IN PRACTICE

As all journeys have an end, the spiritual journey also has an end according to the practice. The ending of the spiritual journey is bound to the external ending of the physical journey of life. In other words, when the person dies, the first part of the journey ends. As the person is coming closer to the final stage of the spiritual journey, the signs may increase. Similar to the fireworks mentioned in the story above, during the last stage of the show, more intense and colorful fireworks may appear.

The moments of experience, life-changing incidents, the avenues of enlightenment . . . All of these signs may come in abundance as the person grows older. Depending on the person's attitude, the person can realize and decode these signs, or move on and perhaps still not understand.

62. The Oppression

There was a man and he had a daughter. The father sometimes used to yell at his daughter and would not allow her to explain herself. One day, the father picked up his daughter from school and again started yelling at her and giving her some unsolicited advice. While they were driving, from out of nowhere, a car appeared next to their car and the father opened the window. The lady driver in the other car was angry and started cursing at the father and even said, "I will have my man find you and kill you." The father did not understand what was going on. He closed his window and kept moving. After a day, the daughter said to her dad, "Dad! I think yesterday, you didn't let me speak and you were yelling at me. God sent this lady from nowhere and she started cursing at you." The father regretfully said, "I think you are right. I am also thinking about that, too."

IN PRACTICE

Everything that happens to the person has a reason. Nothing is random. Nothing is chaos as long as the person knows the meanings. The person should follow the natural laws created by God as a means of respect to God. However, he or she should remember that in a limited human life everything is a sign to improve oneself on the journey and ultimately to better the relationship with Allah. Therefore, miracles are those incidents that break the natural laws to remind the person that everything is under the control of God. For a spiritual person, if the person is attentive, mindful, conscientious, and sincere on the journey, then everything can continuously reveal itself with their miraculous real meanings.

63. Experiential Learning

One day, Owen attended a lecture. There was also a novice religious student who was angry, present. He said, "I don't believe that a spiritual person can be without stress." Owen tried to explain to him, but the student was very disturbed and angry about the problems in his own life. Owen stopped talking, smiled, and observed silence.

IN PRACTICE

Most of the time, it is very difficult to explain the peaceful states of spirituality on the journey to God. Therefore, some of the experts of the path assert that these teachings cannot be taught in a lecture format but should be experienced and lived through practice and worship.

Discussion Question

▶ Why is experience important along with knowledge and practice?

64. The Lost Phone

One day, Hannah was packing for travel and could not find her phone. She checked her car. She checked her handbag. She could not find it. Although she could not imagine traveling without her cell phone and felt uneasy about it, she also thought about how nice travel could be without being bothered by the phone. She remembered that the only person who called her was her husband and he was already traveling with her. In the meantime, Hannah was also trying to understand the possible wisdom behind the evil-seeming incident of losing her phone. Using her husband's cell phone, she texted her own phone. "If you find this phone, please text me." A day later, a person texted that she had found the missing cell phone. After coming back from her trip, Hannah went and picked up the phone. The person who found it was an artist. Hannah gave her a nice gift to thank her for returning the phone. Hannah discovered that had an interest in the artist's themes reflected in her artwork. Now, Hannah understood the wisdom of losing her phone: a possible long-term friendship between Hannah and the artist.

IN PRACTICE

It is important to interpret the evil-seeming incidents with a possible positive outcome graced from God. Sometimes, people's immediate negative response to evil-appearing incidents can ruin their entire life. The notions of patience, wisdom, and reflection should be practiced in all encounters of life.

Discussion Questions

> ▸ Why is it important to interpret everything with their other meanings in practice?
> ▸ How is randomness or chaos understood in practice? Why?

65. The Harsh Voice

There was a person named Bilal in Nisantas, Istanbul, Turkey. When he used to talk to his children, they felt that their father was harsh with them. Realizing this after many years, he started communicating with his children solely by writing on paper and with sign language. His children thought that their father was 'cool', and they started talking about him to their friends. The father was happy because now his children loved him, and they listened to their dad.

IN PRACTICE

It is very important to tune one's voice in communication. It is very important to be in a soft and calm tone with the people of regular interaction like family members and friends. It is very important to maintain a serious tone in interactions of public life, especially in business. The teaching of tuning down one's voice in communication is often mentioned in the verses of the scriptures, in the practices of the prophets, and in the lives of the saints of God. One can see the habit of tuning down one's voice as an imitative way of reaching to the genuine way of practicing calmness, softness, mercy, and caring for the entire creation of God.

Discussion Question

▶ What is the long-term expectation of practicing tuning down one's voice?

66. Oppression and Friends

One day, Diana visited her friends late at night. She was very excited to see them. They chanted nicely, ate snacks, and had a great time. Diana started talking about her achievements since she did not see her friends for some time. After a while, Diana left and went home. She was not able to sleep. Next day, something was bothering her deeply, and she tried to figure out what it was. Finally, she said to herself, "My oppression."

IN PRACTICE

All of the good achievements are given by God to a person. All of the evil outcomes are due to the call of the person and thus evil is created. This is a very fine notion to understand, theodicy, the concept of evil in practice. Therefore, the person should be in enormous gratitude to God by saying, 'thank you God' due to being chosen as a simple means for any type of good. If the person claims any ownership of this achievement, then the person in reality lies and oppresses himself or herself. Every lie spoils and dirties the sweet relationship with God. This can cause the person to feel disturbed, uneasy, and can take the person to a spiritual darkness and misguidance. Therefore, the pronouns 'I' or 'my' are dangerous pronouns which can take the person to oppression, lying, and arrogance. The statements of 'my work', 'I achieved', or similar ones are clearly minefields that can backfire upon the person spiritually due to bragging.

Discussion Question

▶ How can one be selective in using pronouns in daily conversations?

67. The Young Disciples

Ellison used to be quite annoyed with her own children. She thought to herself, "How should I change my perspective about them so that I don't get annoyed with my own kids?" Then, she said to herself, "If I see them as students to be trained on the path, then I will expect everything to be normal."

IN PRACTICE

It is important to raise one's children on a spiritual path. Most of the spiritual teachers raise and train their own children as their own disciples. It is a negligence and mistake if one becomes a teacher for others but not for their immediate kinship groups. The best way of teaching is being a role model and increasing the presence with the disciples. The children become like disciples.

Discussion Questions

- ► What are the traditional methods of raising one's own children in practice?
- ► How can a person balance the roles of being parents and spiritual masters for one's own children?

68. Enemy Advice

There was a woman who wrote her first book. Everyone gave her advice on how to make the book better. Her religious friend gave her advice also on how to improve the book. The author thought that everyone was jealous of her and therefore were criticizing her book. Her friend said to her, "Look! If everyone is saying the same thing about your book, then you should really stop seeing them as your enemies and appreciate what they say and improve it."

IN PRACTICE

It is important not to see people as enemies, haters, or jealousy banks when they give advice. Creating imaginary adversaries only increases one's own arrogance due to not accepting any criticism. It is important to improve oneself even though others may not have a sincere intention when giving advice. Jealousy is always possible and real in practice. There are litanies and prayers to be protected from the evil eye.

Discussion Question

► Why it is difficult to accept criticism from others about oneself?

69. Crooked Advice

One day, Leo asked advice of his friend about helping a person in need. His friend suggested some ways of helping but they did not seem ethical and honest. Leo felt uneasy at the idea of the crooked suggestions. His friend kept insisting that there is nothing wrong if the end result is good, and that it is OK to cheat. Leo kept saying that was not right. The communication went back and forth without any result.

IN PRACTICE

It is important to reach a virtuous act through virtuous and ethical steps. A person gains power and strength from being honest and just in all of his or her affairs. Doing everything ethically with consciousness of God can reward the person in this world and in the afterlife. There are a lot of cases in which a true, honest person may not be appreciated by one's peers, friends, or family members but only truly appreciated by God.

Discussion Question

► How do you explain the above statement 'reaching a virtuous act through virtuous and ethical steps'?

70. The Kids and Candies

Ryan's wife bought boxes of candy snacks for their children to take to school. The snacks were healthy organic ones, but expensive. His wife used to put the candies in the fridge and pantry, accessible to the kids. Quite often Ryan would hear his wife chiding the kids for finishing the snacks at home, leaving nothing for the next day's lunch bags. Ryan listened to her, smiled, and said to himself, "If the candies are accessible then it is normal to finish."

IN PRACTICE

Spiritual candies are given by God as an encouragement for the traveler on the journey. If a person has the choice of getting the candies, then the candies will not survive and finish. Therefore, one should know that all the spiritual candies or miracles are given and controlled by God. The person does not have any control over them unless the person is enabled or empowered by God. This is even true for the prophets. The prophets can show miracles or spiritual candies as long as God empowers them and gives them the ability to do so. Therefore no one can claim ability of divinity except God. In one of the chapters of the scriptures, the prophet mentions his humanness, and that if he knew what would be in the future, then he would increase his good deeds. No one knows the future except God.

Discussion Question

▶ How do you interpret the concept of 'spiritual candies' in your personal life encounters?

71. The Stinginess and the Ice Cream

There was a stingy person named Celia who took her kids and her friend out for ice cream. Her friend was delayed for the ice cream party. She said to herself, "Let me buy the ice cream before my friend comes. If she comes later, she can pay for her own ice cream." She bought the ice cream for her kids and started eating with them. After a few minutes, her friend arrived. Celia was embarrassed and said to her friend, "Let me buy your ice cream too as I promised." Her friend ordered her ice cream. Celia was about to pay for the ice cream when the owner of the store said, "She is on me. You don't need to pay for her." She thanked the owner and felt embarrassed about her thoughts.

IN PRACTICE

It is important to be generous. God gives much to people and does not ask anything in return except the recognition and appreciation of the One and only God. In the above story, Celia had a spiritual sickness of being stingy and fear of spending on others. God sent her a sign, then she felt bad and embarrassed about this issue.

Discussion Question

▶ Why is generosity considered to be virtuous as compared to being stingy?

72. The Long-Haired Brother and the Bald Brother

Thomas had a bald friend. People used to refer to him as the 'brother with bald hair'. This man used to get annoyed with this description until finally he got some surgical hair implants. After a few years, his hair grew long, and people started calling him the 'brother with long hair'. He was now happy and confident about his new nickname. Thomas observed this change in his friend's approach and smiled and said to himself, "What others think; does it matter?"

IN PRACTICE

It is important not to worry about others' opinion, especially if it is related to the externalities. Looks or bodily appearances are one of the traps that people fall in without understanding the essence of the existence of a person. Therefore, there may be some people who may not care what others think. There may be other people who can try to fit into the similar outlook of their culture so that they look normal and ordinary like others.

Discussion Question

► What are different positions in one's outlook in practice?

73. Seeking Guidance

Over many years, Jace was wondering, "Why do some people have guidance and know about God?" One day, she visited one of her friends who was very rich. He was new to the religion. He was so humble that he even saw children as his teachers. Then Jace said, "I found the answer: Humility!"

IN PRACTICE

God can inspire an answer to a question after many years if the person has a genuine struggle and intention of learning. It is not unusual to see stories about a religious master struggling with himself or herself about a dilemma and years later, the answer can be given by God. The concept of guidance in practice appears often with the traits of humbleness and humility. There may be people who can know orthodoxy, the right or authentic path but due to the identity, group ownerships, arrogance or other reasons they may not have orthopraxy, the right practice. Similarly, Satan was very intelligent as mentioned in various scriptures, but he always lost due to his lack of humility.

Discussion Question

► Why do you think humility is one of the important keys for guidance?

74. The Loud Greeter

There was a man who used to greet everyone very loudly in the temple. When this man approached Andrew, he pretended that he was doing his prayers in order not to be disturbed. After a while, everyone in the temple started greeting each other loudly. Andrew smiled and said to himself, "Even though I don't like it, I think this man started something good as a practice. At least people are greeting each other and not grumbling."

IN PRACTICE

It is important to greet each other and smile. The prophets recommend one of the rights of a person over another is greeting each other nicely when they see each other. However, some people, as in the above story, prefer silence and solitude. Andrew avoided socializing but when he saw that the loud greeter encouraged others to increase the practice of greeting, he critiqued and disagreed with his own self and applauded the achievement of the man for starting something good.

Discussion Questions

- ▶ What is the effect of greeting in social life?
- ▶ What is the effect of greeting in spiritual life?

75. Tea for the Traveler

One day, a stranger who was mentally ill visited the temple. Everyone was fasting but the stranger did not know about it. He made tea and wanted to show his generosity and gave a cup of tea to Parker. Parker said that he was fasting. The stranger insisted that he needed to take the teacup from him. Parker did not want to argue and took it from him and put it to the side. He thought to himself, "What is the message?" After a while, a traveler who was not fasting came to the temple looking tired. He said to himself, "Now, I get the message." He gave the tea to the traveler. The traveler was happy, and Parker smiled.

IN PRACTICE

There is a meaning in everything. Nothing is haphazard if a person can understand it. Travelers, the sick, and mentally ill are all exempt from fasting. In the above story, Parker did not want to argue with the stranger who was mentally ill because there was no use. On the other hand, he did not understand why this happened until the traveler came to the temple. Then, Parker found a meaning in this small incident.

Discussion Questions

- ▶ Is it possible to understand the real reason behind every evil or good seeming incident if one is patient?
- ▶ How can one define the notion of 'the real reason' behind every incident?

76. The Sleeping Stranger

There was once a man who had been sleeping at night in the temple for a few weeks. This was a man that people in the temple did not know much about, and they were uncomfortable with this stranger. One day, while only Colton and the stranger were there, Colton approached him and asked if he was the son of a woman who had passed away two weeks ago. The man said, "Yes." Colton said to himself, "Now, everything makes sense." The next day, the man was sleeping in the temple again. One of the administrators of the temple was a harsh man and reprimanded the stranger, saying, "This is a temple. You cannot sleep at night here." Colton witnessed this and felt bad for the stranger. After the prayer finished in the temple, Colton took a courageous step and made an announcement in the temple. He introduced the stranger to everyone and explained why he was sleeping in the temple.

IN PRACTICE

It is very important to have empathy for people. Colton with Divine Guidance understood this sleeping man's situation and guessed that he was the son of the lady who passed away recently. It is common that people need more help and support at the time of loss. Therefore, one can find many instances where people sleep and spend more time in the temples when they are spiritually troubled and in need. In this story, Colton handled the case with wisdom without confronting the harsh administrator directly, but rather addressed the problem to the general audience. This was one of the ways the prophets used to solve any problem and issue among people. The prophets did not target any specific person and accuse them of their mistakes, but tried to teach them with the habit of introducing general guidelines for everyone.

Discussion Question

▶ Why do people tend to have increased quality and quantity of spirituality at the time of loss?

77. Patience

One Friday Ethan was in the temple enjoying his praying and reading the scriptures. There were also three talkative men in the temple. Others in the temple treated them poorly, but Ethan treated them gently and kindly. They knew and liked Ethan and wished to consult him, but they also knew that they should not disturb him while he was reading the scriptures or during prayers. One of the men needed Ethan's attention and sat next to him. In general, Ethan would not let himself be distracted while reading the scriptures, but on this day he responded patiently. The man happily returned to his spot in the temple. When the other two saws how Ethan responded, they were encouraged as well and went next to him one by one. Ethan responded kindly, thinking to himself, "Today is a special day, Friday. I am practicing patience."

IN PRACTICE

If a person is enjoying a nice sweet dessert, he or she may not want to be disturbed. For some senior spiritual people, one's relationship with God in the prayers and reading the scriptures can have the same sweet taste. In the above story, Ethan had that experience with the prayers and reading the scriptures; however, he understood the desire for the three man to talk to him and entertained their conversations. Ethan also realized that he should still continue his engagement with the prayer and reading the scripture after the disturbance by practicing genuine patience.

Discussion Questions

► Is it considered inconsiderate if one does not respond to one's need due to the person's sweet engagement in prayer or worship of God? Why?

► Is it difficult to achieve the level of taking pleasure or sweetness from one's prayers?

78. Accountability, Children, and Milo

One day, the wife of Milo listed all the bad things that their children did. The children were not listening to their mother. The mother felt helpless. Milo said to himself, "If I discipline them, I would be seen as harsh. I won't do anything and will just be silent and watch what happens." Days passed, and the mother became uneasy about the children's abuse, and started to lose control of herself. The house was becoming a chaotic environment. Milo said to himself, "I think I need to do something. Let me act firmly." Milo called the children and listed all their faults that were reported by the mother. There was silence from the children. Milo declared, "One of you needs to sleep upstairs and the other downstairs. You will not sleep in your beds tonight because of what has been happening lately." One went upstairs and the other went downstairs and both children burst out crying. The mother was uneasy, her heart broken. She tried to persuade their father into removing the punishment. Milo remained firm, thinking, "This is similar to people and their relationship with God."

IN PRACTICE

It is important to realize that there is an accountability in this world and in the afterlife. People are at different levels in their ethics and spirituality. Some people may not do evil because they are afraid of its consequence. Others may not do evil because it is not right for them ethically or spiritually. The accountability in the afterlife is necessary for both the affairs of spiritual and worldly engagements. Most elect the spiritual path of performing good actions to avoid evils as classified by God in order to not displease God. They avoid evil because they love God. On the other hand, the lower level travelers, with no blame to them, can perform good and avoid evil due to fear of accountability and the desire for reward. All are good and fine.

Discussion Question

▶ What can be the problems of humanization of the Divine realities in the above case?

79. Terminology of Jealousy

One day Dean went to an interfaith meeting. There were Christians and Muslims, and they were talking about God. The Christian fellow said, "We believe that our God is jealous." The Muslim fellow said, "God does not want anyone to be worshipped except God." They continued debating. Dean looked and smiled and said to himself, "Our Creator is the same. They both say the same thing but in different words and terminologies."

IN PRACTICE

It is very important to worship only God. It is very important to keep proper etiquette and a respectful attitude toward God when one is expressing words and even thinking about God. Therefore, although what is implied with 'jealous' is understood when one is using this word about God, it can also be alienating due to popular human use of this word in negative contexts. One of the parts that religious people should focus upon in their practice is to change terminologies for people in order to approximate them with what they mean all the while with a consideration of keeping the attitude of respect, appreciation, and a humble attitude toward God.

Discussion Questions

- ▶ Why do we have different classifications of relationships with others depending on the people and context such as professional, social, and family relations?
- ▶ How does one expect an appropriate relationship with God similar to the case of different classifications of relationships in a person's life? Why?

80. Joking in Company

One day, Oscar attended an interfaith gathering. There were some discussions about teachers and their level of piety as they are the role models for humans. One of the attendees started explaining one of the teacher's parents' ethical behavior and how parents affect their children. Oscar made a joke about the story, and everyone started laughing. Oscar paused for a minute, horrified. He said to himself, "What did I do? Shame on me!"

IN PRACTICE

Respect beliefs, values, elders, and teachers. Although we are living in a society of jokes, the religious people believe that jokes have limits and should not touch upon sacred items. According to the religious people, the religion, the belief, and the practice is all attitude. In other words, the state of being with God and friendship with God requires maintenance of proper respect. Most of the time, people lose their good friends due to overstepping boundaries. In this case, having respectful boundaries with the sacred— scriptures, teachers, and God—is the key for successful and a regular spiritual journey until one die.

Discussion Questions

- ▶ What should be the balance among the topics selected for joking or fun?
- ▶ Can religious topics be risky as topics of making jokes or fun? Why?

81. Benefit of the Doubt for the Deaf Man

There was a deaf man for whom Arthur felt much compassion. He asked what he could do as work in order to help him. The deaf man mentioned that he could do some cleaning for Arthur, and Arthur accepted. The deaf person did not show up on the promised day. They agreed for another day. He did not show up again. They agreed again for a third time. The deaf man did not show up again. Arthur thought to himself, "I am not going to think that he did not fulfill his promise. I will still make a good excuse for him."

IN PRACTICE

God knows the inside and outside of all things. As humans, we try to help people with our best intention. In the above story, Arthur did not want to think badly of the deaf man. It is important to make or generate good excuses in one's mind in order not to blame people for their faults. This is called 'always thinking good about others'. This attitude is encouraged as a practice as opposed to its opposite. The opposite of this is called 'thinking and assuming always bad about others'.

Discussion Question

► What is the benefit of thinking always good about others?

82. Emotions and Mind

One morning, Bryan was in dispute with his wife. He said to himself, "If I use my mind, I will not burst out with my anger and not discharge myself. I will be better later but not now. If I use my emotions, I will explode and discharge myself. I will feel good now, but will regret and feel terrible later. What should I do?" He was unable to help himself and used his emotions and burst out with his anger, but by midday regretted his choice and said to himself, "I wish I had used my mind."

IN PRACTICE

It is important to use one's mind when emotions and mind are in conflict. Emotions are not always called 'heart' or 'conscience'. The true emotions or inspirations coming from the heart or conscience do not conflict with the mind, logic, and reason. If they are conflicting, then these emotions can be self-generated sources that can lead to evil. At times of conflict, disputes, and anger, these emotions or thoughts can overpower a person's mind, heart, and conscience. One should make their best effort not to be trapped in these temptations in order not to say "I wish" later.

Discussion Questions

- ► Why do we tend to follow our emotions although we know that it is wrong to do so?
- ► In which cases are there benefits or harms of saying "I wish"?

83. Disputes, and Moving On

One day, Mara was in conflict with her husband, and for a few days afterwards her husband was still angry with her. He took the dispute personally and carried his anger. Mara thought, "I should not take it personally but move on." A few days later, everything seemed normal. She said, "Thanks and all appreciation belongs to God."

IN PRACTICE

It is important not to take things personally and expand the conflict more among people, especially between spouses. This notion is much embedded in the scriptures as a suggested way of 'moving on with peace': not taking things too personally in disputes. There are many stories about rulers in religious history whose spouses used to freely criticize and yell at them. These rulers wisely observed silence and patience, especially in family relations.

Discussion Question

▶ In which cases are there benefits or harms from taking things personally?

84. The Bugs and the Belief

One day, there was food at the kitchen table. The mother put a cover on the food to protect it from the bugs. Jay saw it and said to himself, "Wow, this is similar to protecting one's belief from bugs when interacting with others."

IN PRACTICE

It is important to choose people of genuine knowledge and practice with whom to surround oneself. Once a person is with them the person should benefit through all means: presence, observation, and asking questions. If a person is with inauthentic people of knowledge and practice, one should be trained how to filter, what to learn, and what to block.

Discussion Question

▶   Why is it so emphasized to protect one's spiritual valuables?

85. Best Husband Ever!

One day, Finn was taking a walk. He saw a man cutting the grass and caring for his lawn in front of his house. The man wore a shirt on which was written 'Best Husband Ever!' He approached the man, smiled and said, "Nice shirt! Where did you buy it?" The man said, "My wife bought it for me! Look at me! (showing the lawnmower) don't I deserve it!"

IN PRACTICE

It can be easy to make people happy. Especially, in spousal relationships, something that is minor can be a major for the other person. It is interesting to analyze the life of the prophets in his family relations. Everyone was so happy with him. It is narrated that the prophets used to be very relaxed with his family members in order to make them comfortable. He was always in a pleasant mood, smiling and asking about the need of others. Yet, he was taking care of his own personal needs such as stitching his clothes, cleaning, etc. but not asking people's help [2].

Discussion Questions

- ▶ How do you make people happy? What thoughtful things do you say and do?
- ▶ How do people make you happy?
- ▶ What can you do extra to make others happy that you have not been doing?

86. Coffee in Egypt

There was an American married to an Egyptian girl. After getting married, they went to Egypt to visit her family. The girl had some relatives who had a coffee shop in an apartment building where the relatives used to live on the upper floor. After they arrived, the Egyptian wife said to her American husband, "Why don't you hang around with my cousins in the coffee shop and I will go upstairs to see my aunt." The husband was very happy because he liked coffee so much. The cousins hugged the American husband of their relative and treated him with a nice cappuccino. After he finished, they asked if he wanted another cup. The husband said to himself, "I may as well try something else." Then, he wanted mocha. After he drank, out of politeness, they asked if he wanted another one. This continued until the seventh cup. The Egyptian barista got tired and said, "*This is free!*" The husband understood the case and said, "I really appreciate your hospitality."

IN PRACTICE

Everything is *free* given by God. God gives so many things daily—air, health, the ability to see, hear, digest, and even excrete. Yet, we seem to not even recognize them but be ungrateful. Out of all these simple-looking but critical bounties, God only wants recognition from people of the true, only, one and unique Creator Who constantly showers blessings on people [3].

Discussion Questions

- ▶ What are some ways you practice mindfulness in your daily life?
- ▶ What activity do you take time to slow down & really appreciate in your day?
- ▶ How does practicing gratitude help your relationship with God?

87. Harvard

Natalie used to study at Harvard. When she met her friends during the winter break, everyone was talking about her and how she was going to the prestigious and top school, Harvard! Each time they used to say 'Harvard' Natalie used to say *'forgive me God'* in her heart and mind. Then, Natalie said to herself, "Each time they pronounce the word 'Harvard', it is as if the juice of satisfaction is coming from their mouths. I wish they would say *'praise be God'* for the juice of embodiment of perfection of God in their hearts."

IN PRACTICE

It is important to realize how we embody the words. For example, when a person says the word *Harvard* if certain feelings are coming to a person's mind and heart, then this can be called a true embodiment whether it is something right or wrong. Similarly, in spiritual endeavors, the full connection should be there when we say *Praise be God* to fulfill all of our cells with the embodiment of 'perfection of God', 'showing full and true gratitude only to God', 'cleansing oneself from all the dirty and filthy feelings of arrogance and praise of oneself and asking forgiveness from God for these false emotions'. Natalie wished that the people would embody the beneficial divine phrases in their relationship with God instead of the artificial human-made phrases such as *Harvard*. Natalie was saying the phrase *'Forgive me God'* in order to remove from herself any possible filth of arrogance as the people admired Natalie because she was studying at Harvard.

88. The Snake and Ungratefulness

One day, Maria attended a gathering at the park. At the gathering, there were some ungrateful and disrespectful conversations about sacred items such as the divine scriptures. Maria felt uncomfortable being at that gathering. While she was thinking, she saw a garden snake approaching her. Maria said to herself, "This is a sign that I should leave this gathering quickly."

IN PRACTICE

One of the valuables of a person is their relationship with God with the true submission which can be translated as the core of the authentic and true belief. In this case, the person should be more overprotective of this valuable-their *submission*—than of their children or family members, wealth, and other entities that the person is expected to protect. If the person's *submission* is tainted, then the value of the other mentioned things will be tainted. When people have attitudes of ungratefulness, disrespect, and degradation towards the sacred items related with God, one should leave that gathering as Maria did and she even got a sign in order to hasten to leave.

Discussion Questions

- ▶ Have you ever found yourself in a situation where you became uncomfortable with the disrespectful behavior happening in the environment? How did it make you feel?
- ▶ How does that feeling compare with when you are in a gathering of people who respect each other and God?
- ▶ Why do you think it makes a difference?

89. Time Travel

One day, Carter visited his friends. There were a few people in a small room. After chatting with them, there was a silence. Carter was working on his computer. He looked at the others. Everyone was either on their computer or cell phones. Carter said, "If people from 50 years ago came to our time, they would consider us to be weird."

IN PRACTICE

Change is good and appreciated as long as it is good and serving to increase one's relation with God. If it is the opposite, then it is a bad change. One should ask God for help and use one's willpower not to be dragged into the flow of distractions.

Discussion Questions

- ▶ How can I manage my screen time to help myself focus on my real life?
- ▶ In what ways has technology helped me as I continue to develop my relationship with God?

90. The Intentions & the Relations with the Children

Rose used to do her best to please her children. She was excellent to them in order not to be 'the bad guy' but to be the most pleasing person, as a 'friend' with love. Kylie used to please God and accordingly treat her children. She used to sometimes be 'the bad guy', unlike Rose. After a few years, both of their children grew. The children who were treated in the best way with the intention of pleasing them did not turn out with gratitude toward their mother as compared to the other children's attitude toward their parent. The frustrated and mistreated mother said to herself, "What did I do wrong? I did everything to please them."

IN PRACTICE

It is important to make the intention to please God before pleasing people. God can change the hearts of people, can give them love and appreciation for their hearts. If it is done with this intention, then the same close people or engagements can transform as a source of test or trial for us.

91. Heart & the Recognition

Lately, Lila was avoiding all of the social gatherings in order to not be recognized. One day, her husband desperately asked and insisted that she go with him to a social gathering. Lila accepted and said to herself, "I know I will suffer later." She attended the gathering. She was trying to monitor her heart. She realized that there were still remnants of the desire for being recognized. Lila felt very uncomfortable with herself. After she went to her seclusion place, she asked God for forgiveness.

IN PRACTICE

It is very important to constantly struggle and tackle the intrinsic diseases of the heart. One of these diseases is the sickness of being recognized and applauded by people. The ego wants titles, fame, and self-admiration. Yet, these can be spiritual filths similar to, and maybe worse than, urine and other impurities. The person should be in a constant struggle of transforming one's ego to different classifications of the true and happy self.

92. Fair Weather Friends

There were a number of dogs who used to be fed nice food every day by their owner. Among them was a dog called Spot. All the dogs were very happy and proud of their owner including Spot. They held their owner in high esteem. After years of a nice, grateful, and loyal relationship between the dogs and their owner, there were rumors among the dogs in town that the owner was putting some poison in their food. All the dogs started talking about this rumor. Not long after, some of the dogs fed by the owner started talking bad about their owner. This was shocking for Spot. The dogs started leaving their owner. Some of them still stayed with their owner. Spot said to herself, "It is shameful of my friends who left. How can you be fed food all these years and survive, and then, leave your owner due to some rumors?"

IN PRACTICE

We learn from our teachers as they are also humans. The attitude of gratefulness, appreciation, and loyalty towards our teachers should prevail more when our teachers need us even if they make mistakes as humans. Even if they do not make mistakes, it is not uncommon to witness rumors and oppression towards genuine teachers in the past and today. Yet, one can observe the prime projection of this attitude between the person and God. God gives this person so much. One day, an unpleasant or evil-seeming incident touches this person. Then, this person stops his or her relationship with God. What a loss on the person's part! [4]

93. Rewards & End Results

Bryce had children. Each time they would read the scriptures, they would come to their father and mention how much they read and then expect a reward from him. Bryce would then buy them some toys. There was also a wise fool who used to come to the temple and read the scriptures. Each time he read the scriptures, he also used to come to Bryce and mention how much he read and expected a reward from him. Bryce then used to give him a few dollars. He then thought of both cases, and said to himself, "The importance of rewards, encouragement, and necessity for Heaven in the afterlife..."

IN PRACTICE

It is important to do everything to please God. Each person is different in their relationship with God. It is normal to be encouraged and motivated by the end result. This end result can be a toy, a few dollars, or an eternal life in Heaven. Yet, the highest and noblest of these end results is the Pleasure of God.

94. Love On the Way

There were two people—a husband and a wife. One day, the husband got a cut on his limb. The wife gave him a long lecture about how he does not take care of himself well. About a week later, the wife got a cut on her limb in exactly the same spot as her husband. The wife said, "Maybe… my not so nice thoughts about my husband."

IN PRACTICE

When people are close to God, sometimes God can send small warnings with love, kindness, and caring so that they can correct themselves. These nice warnings, like in the above story, are expected to encourage a person to engage in self-reflection.

Discussion Questions

- ▶ Have you ever noticed a loving reminder being sent when your attitude or behavior needed adjustment?
- ▶ Are you grateful and receptive when you receive correction?
- ▶ How can we become more grateful for correction from others, and use it to improve ourselves, our relationships, and our lives?
- ▶ How can we learn to take criticism from others in stride, and not have a negative reaction to it, internally nor externally?
- ▶ How can we learn to be less critical of others?

95. Two Crazy Fools

There were two crazy fools who used to come to the temple to pray and hang around. One was old and the other one was young. The older one used to get angry at the younger one each time he entered the temple and said to him, "Go and wash yourself up before you hang around in the temple. Then come pray." The younger crazy fool used to get upset about this. Yet, due to his respect for the older one, he would wash himself and then start praying. As this continued for some time, the younger one stopped coming to the temple in order to not see the older crazy fool. One day, during a prayer, the cell phone of the older crazy fool started ringing during the prayer. After the prayer was over, the leader gave a long lecture that people should turn off their cell phones during the prayer. The older crazy fool got offended and stopped coming to the temple.

IN PRACTICE

It is important to deliver a message without offending the other person. Although the person may be right, the wrong way of delivering the content can cause sometimes more damage than not delivering the correct content. Although it is difficult, one should train oneself in both perspectives. On another note, one can see the Just attribute of God in the above story. If we offend others, it is likely that someone can offend us as well.

96. The Crazy Fool and the Cleaner in the Temple

One day, Grant was sitting in the temple when the crazy fool arrived. Grant was the only friend of the crazy fool. The crazy fool was upset with everyone, even with his own blood relatives. As usual, Grant offered the crazy fool some nice treats and coffee, but he was acting very formally and was silent with the crazy fool. Then, in came the cleaner of the temple. His name was Jesse. Jesse was a nice guy and silent as well but did not think much of the crazy fool. The crazy fool started chatting with Jesse about the weather and life. After a few minutes of nice conversation, the crazy fool burst into his normal, real self and started complaining about life and people. Jesse was not able to stop him. The crazy fool was talking incessantly. Jesse needed to go back to his job of cleaning the temple. He was not able to do so because the crazy fool was talking angrily without pause and shouting about people and life. Grant was watching this and he said to himself, "This is the reason why I am acting formally."

IN PRACTICE

It is important to try to understand the personalities of different people and their specific needs so as to know how to approach them. A person can help another person in different ways without exposing them in their weaknesses. Grant knew about the crazy fool. He pretended to act formally in order to not put him in an uncomfortable situation of being humiliated by others. Yet, he still treated him nicely. Grant was his only friend in life. God has bestowed on the genuine religious people the skills to be good friends with everyone including the people or animals who are disliked or scary. There are stories about religious people being friends with snakes and lions as well.

97. Complaints & Lack of Appreciation

Tucker used to constantly receive complaints from his wife. His wife always said that Tucker did not do anything around the house. She is the one always doing everything. Tucker used to ask, "What do you want me to do? Please tell me explicitly." His wife used to give the 'to-do list' and he used to complete it to the best of his ability. Then, his wife used to be happy. After a while, his wife again started to say same things. Tucker again asked for the explicit 'to-do list'. Then, she was happy again. This cycle continued.

IN PRACTICE

Complaints do not add value but increase resentment for everyone. In family, professional, or other relationships, some people may do more work as compared to others. This can be a fact. On the other hand, the ones who seem to do more work should not act as 'the savior', and yet, at the same time, the ones who do less work should express their appreciation for the hard workers and try to contribute as much as they can regardless of the other party's complaints. Establishing relationships and doing things to please God can minimize or eliminate resentments when people appreciate the person's efforts.

98. Eschatology, Necessary and Unnecessary Engagements

Alyssa was eating food with some friends. Her friends opened a discussion about the cases of eschatology, and the possibilities about the End of Days. Her friends were very interested in the topic, but not Alyssa. Alyssa said to herself, "Every learning engagement should have a good purpose. Mere curiosity of learning something without any purpose can induce fear, anxiety, and distraction in the mind and heart."

IN PRACTICE

It is important to learn and engage in any conversation or a lecture with a purpose and an aim. Mere engagements of chatting or hanging around may cause the person's mind to wander and become distracted. The prophets asked for protection from the knowledge that does not benefit the person. On the other hand, one can learn and inquire about topics such as eschatology with a purpose and an aim. These can be, for example, normalizing the occurrences and changes in societies through predicted prophetic miracles, and possibly using these avenues to explain to people that changes in our lives or societies are not random, but rather all are under the control and knowledge of God.

99. Real Teachers Do Not Judge

There was a teacher who was so gentle, kind, and forgiving of people's mistakes. Patrick used to learn a lot from this teacher. Yet, he was still making mistakes about not judging others and being kind and gentle in a manner similar to his teacher. Patrick said to himself, "It is very difficult, yet I try to be like my teacher."

IN PRACTICE

As humans, we make mistakes. All of the prophets as genuine teachers had this non-judgmental quality. The prophets were very kind and gentle teachers and implemented this gentleness and kindness in human relations constantly, whereas we tend to immediately rush to judge people in our relationships. This is the biggest difference between regular spiritual folks and the highest role models. Yet, we strive to be similar to our role models.

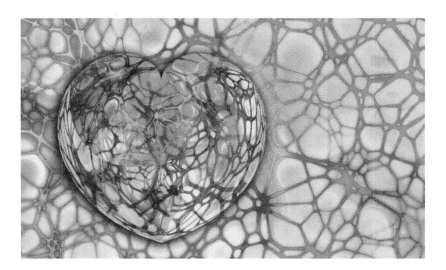

100. Marriage Proposal

Myles was not married. He happened to see a girl and fell in love with her. Then, after many days and weeks of the pain of love, he tried to find a way to find out if she was interested in getting married to him. Then, there was an arrangement made to meet with her. Myles said as soon as he saw her, "Will you please marry me? I love you so much." The girl said, "Yes." Myles started jumping up and down because of his happiness. The girl said, "I just want to say I have a sister who is more beautiful than me." He said, "Are you kidding me? Where is she?" The girl said, "Look there." Myles turned his face and died immediately. The girl said, "The real lover does not turn his gaze from the loved one even for a second."

IN PRACTICE

We claim to love God. Yet, our focus or gazes are all over the place expecting benefit and return from others. We prepare our spiritual death when we unfocus ourselves from God [5].

101. The Inviter

There was a man whom Zane used to call the Inviter. This man used to invite others for good and beneficial programs, but he did not attend himself. It was again one of those days and the Inviter came to Zane and said, "There is a great beneficial lecture now in the other temple if you want to go." Zane thanked him politely for the invitation and smiled because as usual the Inviter did not go to this great program himself but was inviting others to it.

IN PRACTICE

Actions come before words. Representation does not need words. People have minds to think and deduce meanings. Great orators do not have value as long as they do not practice. God values the sincere efforts but not cheap words [6].

102. Firing the Cleaner of the Temple & Disappointment

There was an old man who used to clean the temple. He did not speak English. Yet, he was good friends with Jeremy, and they used to speak in sign language. One day, the old man came to Jeremy very sadly and told him that he received a letter from the administration stating that his cleaning position would be terminated after 30 days. Jeremy felt sad and talked to the administration but unfortunately, there was no change in their decision. During these 30 days, the old man came to Jeremy a few times a week and said the same thing-that his position will be terminated by the end of the month. Jeremy felt very sad and he said to himself, "I wish we could place our expectations only on God, and not on people."

IN PRACTICE

As humans, we expect recognition and encouragement from others, especially, if a person has been working in a place for a long time. Instead of recognition, the person is fired with only 30 days' notice. Due to the temporal and mortal nature of humans, their giving worth to other humans may have limited and temporal values. Humans can seem to applaud or congratulate others for their achievements, but it is all time-based, superficial, and periphery. If the person expects recognition only from the Infinite God, then his or her achievement transforms to be infinite—and not time-based or temporal as compared to human achievement—in an infinite reward system of Heaven.

103. The Farewell Visit of the Temple Cleaner

It was the last day for the cleaner of the temple. After he finished cleaning the temple, he came to Oscar. Oscar said to him, "Please forgive me," and gave him a small gift. The temple cleaner was surprised because for a long time spanning many months and even more than a year, the cleaner had never heard Oscar talking and they had always communicated in sign language. Oscar smiled and the man left. Oscar was sad with all of the good memories he shared with the temple cleaner.

IN PRACTICE

It is important to ask for forgiveness from the people with whom we interact. The possibilities of backbiting and taking away the rights of others are serious engagements that require accountability in front of God in the afterlife. Therefore, it is traditional to ask forgiveness in farewell cases although there may not be an issue among the individuals [7].

104. Carrying Change

Preston used to not like to carry change and cash in his pocket. He liked to have empty pockets without any weight. One day, a beggar came to him and asked him for money. He felt bad that he could not help him. The next day, while he was out another beggar came and asked him for money. He again felt bad that he could not help him. Finally, Preston said, "Maybe I should carry change in my pocket." The next day, he went out. He was happy that he had change so that if a beggar were to come and ask for money from him, he had something to give to the person. All day went by and no beggar came. Preston felt sad.

IN PRACTICE

There are opportunities, times, and engagements for each place and time. There are five-times prayers that need to be performed during a certain time frame. People fast during a certain month. They go to pilgrimage at a certain time. If these times pass, opportunities to fulfill that good deed are missed. Similarly, in the above story, although Preston can get a reward from God due to his intention, it is always important to be prepared to catch the opportunities at the right times in one's relationship with God.

105. Effects of the Society and Humanness

Morgan as usual was practicing her life of solitude and minimal interaction with people. She sometimes used to think she really didn't care what was happening in the world as long as she could maintain her relationship with God. One day, an epidemic disease came to the world. The news about it was everywhere every day. Morgan still maintained her solitude with God without being very affected. Yet, as she was hearing the news in her minimal interaction with people, she said to herself, "As a human, it is very difficult to guard yourself from the effects of society, although one can try to minimize all the social nearness."

IN PRACTICE

A person on the path is not disturbed with the daily occurrences of scandal perspectives of news. One can see a lot of people living with the news, sleeping with the news, and waking up with the news in front of them on their TVs, cell phones, and computers. They let this news navigate their emotions up and down, cracking them apart and destroying them. Yet, a person on the path has a goal, meaning, and purpose in life. Daily occurrences or scandal news do not navigate their emotions. Therefore, the people on the path engage themselves with the useful knowledge and information as suggested by the prophets to help their lifelong goal on the path. This goal is to be happy, calm, and serene in this life by pleasing the One who is the Source of all happiness, calmness, and serenity.

106. High Expectations and Children

Max had eight children. He used to love the seventh one so much. One day, the seventh one made a big mistake in his life. Max was so disappointed and was not able to make peace with himself about this major mistake of his child. Then, he said to himself, "I should not really sanctify any human being, even my loved ones!"

IN PRACTICE

Humans are humans. Understanding this reality is important. If a person sanctifies or divinizes another human being, this is one of the highest mistakes that one can make in their life. God requires only attaching oneself truly to God. One can love someone or something, yet true and correct valuation of everything is important. In the above story, one of the common mistakes is the parents' false and wrong assessment and valuation about their children. Then, when a parent witnesses the invalidation of their assessment, they can experience big frustration and devastation of their expectations. One should always expect from God. God is the only One Who does not leave the person with any frustration [8].

107. Good Intentions and Finding Yourself in a Mess

One day, Sydney wanted to help her friend who was in need. She was trying to be extremely careful about how she should help her so that her friend would not get offended. Her friend was a type who did not want any help from anyone. Sydney gently tried to approach her, yet she got angry and said some harsh words to her. Sydney was upset and holding herself not to say anything back. She said to herself, "You never know how something can become a mess!"

IN PRACTICE

God rewards the person according to their intention but not according to the outcome of what they achieve or lose. Sometimes, a person with a good intention can find himself or herself in an unexpected situation. Yet, maintaining one's composure, calmness, and patience and not acting with anger can always be more fruitful in both spiritual and worldly affairs.

108. Winners and Losers

One day, Jax gained a lot of knowledge, piety, and respect. He started to have a lot of followers changing themselves with the aid of his teachings on the path of God. Jax's friends and family members were also benefiting from his knowledge and teachings. They said to themselves, "We are so lucky that we have Jax in our lives. What a great bounty of God! It is like winning a lottery!" Yet, a few of his old friends and family members got jealous and said, "Why him? We are better than Jax. Why don't people follow us, but they follow him?" They became increasingly jealous of him. They lost on the path of winning.

IN PRACTICE

It is important to detect our spiritual diseases before they kill us. A person on the path of God can be winning yet he or she can lose with jealousy. An intelligent person can realize that if God chooses some people to be role models, such as the prophets and saints, then an intelligent person can make use of this to benefit their own spiritual growth. An intelligent person benefits from the people who are the source of light and guidance as the friends of God. Killing oneself with jealousy and self-destructive hatred is the worst foolishness, absurdity, and irrationality. When one reviews the life of the prophets, everyone boosted their true spirituality with their pearl and diamond teachings. Yet, there were a few from their old friends and family members who blocked themselves due to their iron curtains built with jealousy, hatred, and arrogance in their hearts [9].

109. The Ban

One day, Daisy heard that the town banned people from going out at night due to expected protests and vandalism. She said to herself, "People will be in fear even if nothing happens." She spent her night in regular chants, prayers, and remembrance of God.

IN PRACTICE

It is important not to be trapped in current events [10]. The maintenance of the relation with God can put the person in peace and calmness even during times when many people are in the states of fear and panic. At these times, it is a responsibility to give people hope and calmness once one takes care of oneself spiritually with one's regular engagements in one's relationship with God. The one who is already in the flow of fear and panic cannot help others already dragged down with daily and hourly news of magazines.

110. Head of the State & the Poor Man

There was a poor man in the temple suffering from paranoia. Every day, he used to come to Knox in the temple and tell him how everyone in the temple is planning against him. One day, as usual, this poor man came to Knox and said to him, "Were you here when the head of the state came yesterday? He came here to plot against me with others in the temple. I am a citizen of this country. They cannot kick me out." Knox did not say anything as usual and offered him a coffee.

IN PRACTICE

Sometimes, our ungrounded fears about others overwhelm us and make us dysfunctional [11]. If this happens constantly, then it can become an illness referred to as persecution complex or paranoia which can lead to psychosis. Yet, it is important to diagnose it in its early stages before it becomes an illness. On the spiritual path, having a good spiritual teacher, a good collective meditation group, a good friend, and daily regular personal spiritual practices can be some of the means to detect and remove the seeds of these diseases before they grow further. Reliance on God constantly, removing and discharging oneself from all fears and anxieties with chanting and regular daily prayers can be some of the practical remedies that can prevent building plaque on the heart and mind causing emotional and mental disorders.

111. Silly Things Turn Into Big Problems

One day, Kaden was thinking about how simple and silly things can cause big problems if they are not handled gently and with wisdom and patience. He said to himself, "Anything at work, at the temple, at home and even with friends. Wow! Very challenging, yet it looks like a piece of cake! Maybe, it should be called a *piece-of-cake looking minefield!*"

IN PRACTICE

The notion of temptation can be defined as chaos in societies, in families, and even in any type of relationship. The starting point of temptations can be something silly and it can grow if it is not handled carefully and taken care of with wisdom and patience [12]. Some contemporaries may refer to this as early stage cancer cells as compared to the ones in the later stages that can kill people as they kill relationships. They can cause social, family, kinship and friendship chaos, aggression, violence, animosity, and disconnected relationships or diasporas at group or community levels. Therefore, the person should not take anything easy or as a 'piece of cake' in life but remain always in the state of uncertainty. Yet, at the same time, it's important to also stay in the state of tranquility by praying to God for protection and striving to have a very strong relationship with God regularly.

Discussion Questions

▶ What do you do in your life to address small problems before they grow into big problems? At work? At school? At home? In relationships?

▶ How do you manage your stress as you strive to balance the many aspects of your life?

▶ Do you notice a connection between how much care you are putting into your spiritual life and how well you are able to manage your daily stresses?

112. Simple is Better

There was a Turkish person married to an American person. One day, the Turkish person was at home with her kids. She made macaroni for her children and made it in Turkish style with mint, diced tomatoes, olive oil and salt. After that she served to the kids. All the kids were asking for ketchup and hot sauce. She insisted that they needed to eat in the way that she made it with her style. The kids started crying and said, "If our dad was here, he would give us whatever we want. We don't want to eat plain macaroni." She said, "Either you eat it this way, or no food!" After the kids ate the food, they started saying among themselves, "Wow! This is the best macaroni we have ever eaten although it looked plain and it was much healthier!"

IN PRACTICE

Sometimes, we cry and ask for something from God in such a way that we are very confident about our position. In the end, we become disturbed and ungrateful in our relationship with God because the result is not in the way that we wanted. After many years, we start seeing the benefits of God-given results over the ones we deemed good and desired to have. Then, at that point in time, if we have not lost our sense of gratitude, we apologize to and ask forgiveness from God. But, all those years between the disconnection from and the re-connection with God could have been wasted in misery and darkness. Yet, if we develop the attitude of gratitude and constant reliance on God, all the years, months, days and even minutes can be spent in constant sweetness and tranquility [13].

Discussion Questions

- ▶ Discuss a time when something worked out better than you had expected, and you looked back at the time spent worrying and knew you had wasted that time feeling that way. How do you wish you would have spent that time instead?
- ▶ Was there ever something in life you really wanted only to find out later that it was not as good for you as you thought it was going to be?
- ▶ Have you grown to appreciate something in your life for becoming more than you expected it to be when it first came into your life?
- ▶ Have you had any experiences of feeling like you received just what you needed, right when you needed it, even if it weren't exactly what you would have preferred?
- ▶ Have you ever had the experience of feeling, "That's just what I needed!" after something has happened to help take care of you, make your day better, or nurture you in some way that you didn't even know you needed until after it happened?
- ▶ How have these experiences affected your sense of gratitude to God and faith in God?

113. Child and the Parents

One day, Lacey visited a family and witnessed an interaction between the child and parents. The child said to the parents, "You did not do anything for me. I don't care about you." The mom said, "Oh my son! Do you remember the days that I used to change your diapers, breastfeed you, and take you to your school? Do you remember the days that your dad used to take care of you, teach you, and get what you needed?" The child said, "I don't care. I don't want to know you in my life." Lacey did not like the environment and said to herself, "What an ungrateful child! This is exactly the same and the worst case—when the person does not recognize God and is ungrateful to their Creator."

IN PRACTICE

It is required to respect, acknowledge, and appreciate the parents regardless of if they are good or bad. Even in disputes of religion, God orders their kind treatment in the scriptures. The relationship of the person with their parents can be a measuring stick for the people to judge their relationship with the Creator. The Creator, God, has more rights on a person than the parents. Yet, there are a lot of people who tend to deny these rights.

114. Vanilla Ice Cream and the Sufi

Ahmed was from Turkey who had a hard time pronouncing the word vanilla and yet, he loved vanilla ice cream. In Turkish, there are no letters differentiating the sounds between *w* and *v*. Again, one day, Ahmed went to a drive-thru to buy ice cream for his kids and himself. He said, "Can I please get three baby cone vanilla ice creams?" The cashier on the speaker at the drive-thru said, "Sir, what did you want, could you repeat it again?" He repeated himself, but again, the cashier didn't understand. After a few times of going back and forth, the cashier said, "Sir, sorry, I think we have some problem at our speaker system. Sorry for the inconvenience. If you could kindly pull up to the window, we can take your order there."

IN PRACTICE

It is always preferred to assume good for others. Although the person may know others' mistakes and spiritual diseases, it is a spiritual level and maturity to gently address these issues without directly pointing or blaming the person. In the above story, the cashier gently addressed the problem without making Ahmed feel bad.

Discussion Questions

- ▶ Give an example of how you might politely address someone's misbehavior without embarrassing the person.
- ▶ Give an example of how someone has politely addressed your misbehavior without embarrassing you.
- ▶ What is the benefit of assuming the good for others? How does that benefit others and how does it benefit you?

115. The Mirrors & the Kids

One day, Nola was thinking about which of her kids she is most similar to in character. She had three children. After a while of thinking hard, she said, "My childhood is similar to the youngest one. My present character is similar to the middle one. Perhaps, my old age character will be similar to the oldest one."

IN PRACTICE

It is important to realize that God is fair and just. God sends us people, events, or things to see our own selves. Yet, we do not seem to take lessons from them but rather see them as external events, or things related with others. One of the biggest mirrors among them is a person's own children [14].

Discussion Questions

▶ What have your children taught you about yourself?
▶ Who else in your life acts as a mirror for you?

116. Train Ride Nowhere

One day, Elliot was riding on the train in Boston. It was rush hour in the morning. She was calmly sitting on the train, disconnecting from her surroundings and engaging in meditation. She then for a second put her head up and realized everyone was looking at their cell phones and they were also disconnected from their surroundings. Then, Elliot smiled and said to herself, "Orthodox and post-modern spiritual looking people."

IN PRACTICE

Disconnection from one's physical medium is a virtue as long as this is disconnection takes the person to a better spiritual state. If the disconnection aggravates the person's focus with more distraction, one should reconsider the effects of this disconnection. In the above story, cell phones can be tools for the representations of the modern spiritual-looking engagements.

Discussion Questions

▶ What are some ways the cell phone can be used to promote a better spiritual state?
▶ What are some other activities that could be done on a train ride to promote a better spiritual state?

117. The Temple Administrators

One day, Griffin was traveling. He visited a temple during his travel. He said to himself, "Let me go to the early morning prayer and stay there for a few hours to do my meditation." After the morning prayer was over, the administrators of the temple came over to Griffin and said that they needed to close the temple.

IN PRACTICE

It is important to help the travelers and use the prayer places for their suggested purpose by the prophets. Unfortunately, there are a lot of people who seem to follow the policies of institutions but do not follow genuinely and mercifully the pearl and diamond teachings of the prophets.

118. Bee Confident

There was a confident person named Kyle who used to give advice about bees. He used to say, "As long as you don't bother the bees, they don't sting you." One day, he went out into the backyard with his wife to sit in the gazebo. There was a bee around his wife. His wife got very nervous and agitated. Kyle said, "As long as you don't bother the bees, they won't sting you." He smiled confidently and the bee left. One day, Kyle was walking under a tree and he heard a buzzing sound around his neck. He got nervous and started thinking, "If this bee stung me on my neck, I could be hospitalized." Then, he panicked and put his hand on his neck, and immediately felt the pain. The confident Kyle was stung by a bee. He smiled bitterly to himself, changed slightly his usual motto and said, "As long as you don't fret and panic when the bees are around, *then* they don't sting you."

IN PRACTICE

In spiritual journeys and life endeavors, sometimes rush or panic modes can cause more damage than an expected benefit due to the rushing or panicking. The prophets suggest being passive and not active in those times of uncertainty even though there can be an expected benefit. In the scriptures, it is mentioned that the long-term harms of rushing to take action can be more damaging than short-term explicit harms [15].

119. Monitoring the Heart

Lenore used to teach the elite of the society. She was trying to control her heart within the position and among the prestigious identities of her students. As she was trying to monitor her heart for any type of disease, she felt some type of anxiety, fear, and uneasiness before and after teaching her students. She understood and detected this sickness and said to herself, "The viruses are entering into my heart. That is the reason why I feel uneasy and fearful. I need to practice more detachment."

IN PRACTICE

The person always makes one's intention to please God. If this intention is slightly affected by other means, then the person can immediately be diseased. The initial symptoms of this disease can be fear, anxiousness, and uneasiness. One should constantly go back to the embodiment of detachment phrases and physical prayers accompanied with tears to clean the filth. If this cleaning is not done regularly and immediately, the disease can spread into all of the spiritual faculties. Therefore, there is no guarantee of one's pure and full relationship with God until after one dies. The person should be in a constant state of spiritual alertness and monitoring of their heart.

120. Password & Keeping Secrets

There was a small girl who used to tell others about her family life incidents as were related to her parents and siblings. Her mother, Monica, used to advise her that there are things that should remain only within the family, that others do not need to and should not know. One day, this girl's cousin came to see her. They used to be best friends. While the two girl-cousins were playing together next to Monica outside, the wind closed the door of the house. The guest-cousin needed to go inside the house to get a drink of water and asked her cousin, "Can you please tell me the passcode so that I can go inside?" The girl went to her mom and said in a whispering voice, "Should I tell her?" The mom smiled and said, "This is not a secret. She is your cousin. She can go inside the house."

IN PRACTICE

There are many secrets that one should keep with God. Exposing them can make the person lose that intimate, trust-based relationship. Similarly, in a family, among husband, wife, and children there can be some secrets. Exposing them to others can make the people lose the close relationships and break the trust among them. Secrets with God and others are all trusts that one should not betray [16].

121. Prescriptions for the Heart

Peter used to have a hard time understanding people and treating them accordingly. It took him one year to understand a person. Another person, it took two years for Peter to understand. There are ones whom he still does not understand. Peter said to himself, "Once you understand them, then you can treat them accordingly."

IN PRACTICE

Sometimes, we do not understand our differences related to gender, age, and culture. We insist on our stance without contextualizing the differences and normalizing them. Once the person normalizes the seeming differences, then the empathy can develop. Genuine empathy can lead to genuine communication, helping others, and learning from others. The prophets always used to give different answers to the same question for different people as the ultimate embodiment of empathy, kindness, and gentleness.

122. See No Evil

Greta was watching a cartoon with her kids on a Saturday night. They were eating popcorn, ice cream, and melted nacho cheese with crackers. Everyone seemed to enjoy watching. Yet, Greta was critically thinking about the representations in the cartoon. She said to herself, "What if my kids see similar looking people on the street? They will all be scared. Representations!"

IN PRACTICE

Our memories are built through our minds and hearts and they are not garbage. We cannot watch things and then not think about their consequences. Every piece of spiritual garbage inhaled, seen, heard, or experienced will affect our lifelong memories in this life and in the afterlife. Looking, seeing, and watching are all bounty from God. If this bounty is not used with other ones in their properly prescribed ways, then they will be witnessing against us as mentioned in the scriptures.

Discussion Questions

▶ In what ways has your media consumption negatively informed your views of stereotypes?
▶ Do you avoid any types of media as part of your spiritual lifestyle?
▶ How might you use media to enhance your relationship with God?

123. Our God First

One day, Jayda attended an interfaith gathering. She said our God is the Same, One, and Unique Creator whether we say God, Elohim, or Allah. All the beautiful and perfect names belong to God. There were some who wanted to emphasize that their God was different. Jayda said to herself, "I don't know why we are jealous of sharing our One and Unique Creator and getting into these lowly identity issues and problems."

IN PRACTICE

First, it is important to find common ground and shared values and beliefs before one discusses the differences. Being so excited about talking about differences can indicate some spiritual diseases such as jealousy and arrogance. This can be very dangerous in the discourses of religious topics and discussions both in this world and in the afterlife.

124. Talking About or to God?

One day, Ashlynn attended a spiritual retreat. The retreat was about relationships with God. One of the speakers said, "I think we have talked sufficiently about God. Now, let us talk *to* God through prayer." Ashlynn said to herself, "Wow! This is an interesting statement." Then, she started thinking about this statement.

IN PRACTICE

It is interesting to realize that sometimes a person or especially a genuine teacher makes a statement and it really makes a mark on the person's heart and mind. This one simple-looking statement can lead to a lot of spiritual openings for the person. Most of the time, it is not due to the skills of an eloquent speaker but the power or heaviness of the words, phrases, or statements coming from the heart of the person and penetrating the hearts of others. As one looks at the life of the prophets, they said few words in conversations. Yet, it was sufficient to transform individuals and societies. The unfortunate ignorant and naive witnessed this transformation but they did not rationalize the power of this change and called the prophets or genuine teachers as magicians.

125. Remembrance

Elizabeth used to go to the Boston airport for work every Wednesday. She used to get a cup of hot water to make her own coffee with chants from a coffee shop at the airport. There was a cute Chinese bartender. Each time Elizabeth went and offered money, she used to say, "That is okay. No money needed." The airport was extremely busy every day with thousands of people. After a few weeks, Elizabeth went again on a Wednesday. She asked again for a cup of hot water and tried to hand over the credit card as usual although the bartender did not charge any money. This time the bartender said, "We can't give you this for free every day," but still she did not charge for the hot water. Elizabeth smiled and left and said to herself, "The importance of regular prayers!"

IN PRACTICE

It is important to practice the prayers and rituals regularly. God accepts and gives the reward of prayers as if the person spent in one worship to another with the Divine Mercy and Grace. In the above story, although Elizabeth went to the coffee shop every Wednesday, the bartender thought that she was coming every day due to the regularity. On a positive note, she remembered her among hundreds of people visiting the coffee shop.

126. The Man of Gratitude

Sultan used to know a man for many years. He always used to say, "Many thanks and all gratitude is to God." One day, this man had a big accident and he was about to die. Sultan went and saw the man. The man said to Sultan, "Many thanks and gratitude to God." After a year, Sultan saw this man again. He had brain surgery. He was almost going to die due to internal bleeding in his head. The man said to Sultan, "Many thanks and gratitude to God." After a few more years, the man got older. Sultan saw the man again. The man had a stroke and he was hardly able to talk. The few words that the man was able to utter to Sultan were, "Many thanks and all of the gratitude to God." Sultan started crying on the spot!

IN PRACTICE

It is important to embody thankfulness, gratitude, and appreciation to God. This life is a test to reveal the levels of people in their degree of gratitude to God. Some of us can complain with a small pin pain on our body due to an accident and immediately blame God questioning why God did not protect us. Some exceptional people like the man in the above story can embody gratitude and thankfulness for God. God appreciates and prepares great rewards for the ones who excel in this test of recognition and remain always grateful to God.

127. Reminders & Blame

Remy used to remind people before bad things happened so that people could do something to fix the issues before they happened. When a problem had already happened, she used to not remind them, but rather try to console the people and make them feel at ease. A friend of hers asked, "Why don't you remind them that you told them before about the possible problems?" Remy said, "If I tell them after the problem occurs, then it is called blame, and not a reminder. The reminder is the advice before something happens so that people can take some precautions."

IN PRACTICE

The prophets did not blame people when people did not listen to their advice. They instructed them with reminders before incidents occurred, but afterwards he did not blame them. There are many incidents of this principle. There were even cases when people faced very dire outcomes due to not listening to the prophets. After the incident, the prophet did not say even once, "I told you, but you didn't listen." In every aspect of life, our role models such as the prophets teach us how to be a real human being without breaking people's hearts.

128. Real Sincerity & Fame

There was a writer named Jayden. One day, Jayden met another person named Ace who was in practice. Ace had a very interesting life story of change. He tried different ways of spirituality before becoming a spiritual person. Ace said to Jayden, "You can write my life story. Maybe, it may inspire others. In case it becomes famous and one of the top reads, I do not want to be known. Please do not use my name or any identifiers so that in case people want to backtrack to me, they won't figure out that it is my biography."

IN PRACTICE

Sincerity is the key. Everything is performed to please God. All the efforts of inspiration are performed to please God. In this case, fame in the efforts of inspiring others can be poisonous. The natural human tendency can be eagerness to become famous to inspire others in order to please God. Yet, this can be one of the traps on the path. To avoid this trap, the person should really seek and ask, "How can I be unknown by all humans and known only by God, and yet inspire others towards goodness?" This is the real sincerity. Humanly recognitions, titles, and fame are valueless and even they can be a spiritual poison for the person. Unidentified, unnamed, and unknown engagements by humans are spiritually safer and more sincere than their opposite that attract other lowly intentions and motivations.

129. The Mother and Colin

One day, Colin visited his mom. He mentioned to his mom about the genuine practice. His mom got angry and cursed his teachers. Colin started crying and went to his teacher and explained what happened. He asked his teacher if he could pray for his mom. Then the teacher started praying for her. Then, Colin went to his home. He knocked on the door. The mom opened the door and apologized about what she did. She said, "Can you please teach me the spiritual practice? I need it in my life."

IN PRACTICE

The prayers of teachers for the students are very effective. God can easily answer these prayers as compared to other relationships. There is no interest-based relationship between the teacher and student. In the genuine practice, they engage with their roles of teaching and learning in order to please God.

130. The Man of Forgiveness

One day, Clayton was traveling to Toronto, Canada. He stopped by a temple to pray. A man from elsewhere led the prayer and not the customary prayer leader. After the prayer, the man said from nowhere, "Please ask God's forgiveness an abundance of times and don't be angry." Clayton said to himself, "He is talking to me."

IN PRACTICE

God can inspire people and even send angels in the form of humans to address their dilemma if they are trying on the path of God sincerely and trying to be aware of their inner voices or dialogues. It is not uncommon in the tradition that individuals show up from nowhere to address the need of a person. It is not uncommon in the tradition that the teachers or friends of God address from nowhere the problems of the person in a lecture. Yet, one should take heed of it and change oneself and appreciate the One constantly Who sends these reminders.

131. The Wise Fool and the Locked Doors

There was a wise fool who used to sometimes act as a fool and sometimes as wise. When he used to act wisely, people let him enter the temple. When he used to act foolishly, people did not let him enter the temple. Rafael was observing this incident. Each time the wise fool was on probation of not entering the temple due to his foolishness, he used to come to the temple and the temple door would be locked. Rafael was inside by himself in the temple. Each time, the wise fool used to come the locked doors. Sometimes he opened them although the wise fool did not have the keys for these doors. Rafael first used to get startled about it while observing this, but then he tried to normalize it and tried to understand the wisdom behind it.

IN PRACTICE

The people who are loved by God are hidden. It is very critical not to treat any person harshly and break their hearts. Especially, if they are loved by God, then the person may take the risk of attracting the displeasure of God on oneself. This can be very dangerous even this person who causes uneasiness for others is another Friend of God. Another point is that the places of worship are venues for people to discharge themselves and connect with God. We do not have authority to ban people from entering these places. In the above story, the wise-fool was a hidden person perhaps loved by God. God enabled him to enter this place of worship beyond the physical means.

132. Sharing and Caring: Food

Ember had four kids. One of the kids did not want to share his food but if someone ate his food secretly, he did not care. Another kid did like to share his food but if someone ate her food secretly, she got very angry and started screaming. There was another kid who did not like to share her food and became extremely angry when someone ate her food secretly. There was another kid who did like to share his food and did not care if someone ate his food secretly. Ember loved the last one the most and said to herself, "I wish even some adults can be like him, a very good quality!"

IN PRACTICE

Our real character reveals itself when we are tested with the application of these sublime teachings on the path of God. There are a lot of people who preach and listen to preachers and even cry. Yet, when it comes to application, they are not really aware of their own selves.

133. Galaxies and the Person

One day, Danna attended a gathering. There was an attendee who was discussing the galaxies. There was another attendee who disagreed with the argument and she emphasized the importance of the self in one's own inner journey rather than the outer journeys of spiritual traveling. The teacher was watching the conversation and said, "Both are important to break the attitude of heedlessness and 'I don't care' for different people. It can also be important for the same person who may be going through different conditions with different spiritual states."

IN PRACTICE

It is important to recognize the different avenues given by God to break our attitudes of unrecognition and unappreciation in our relationships with the Divine. Sometimes, the realization of stars, the moon, and galaxies and sometimes a feeling coming from simple human engagement can help the person to break this heedlessness. A person in different states of spiritual engagement can benefit from each at different times. Different people with different spiritual tastes of engagements can benefit differently from each of the available resources.

134. Good Company

One day, Leona was thinking about the reason for her fears, uneasiness, and feelings of insecurity. She was thinking about this for a long time. Then, she visited some good friends. They did a group chant and reading. She felt super happy, calm, and refreshed. All of her fears were gone. She said to herself, "My need for good company!"

IN PRACTICE

It is very critical to be around good company of friends and teachers from whom the person can benefit from their experiential knowledge on the path of God. A person can be a genius, a good reader, and a critical thinker. Yet, a human is a human. They need good people to receive different frequencies of goodness from their experience.

135. Dual Identities

Arlo used to immediately detect the ill feelings in himself towards others. One day, he felt the feelings of jealousy towards some people. He immediately caught it and started the work, struggle, and process of terminating these feelings and transforming them into better and positive ones. Another day, a person came to Arlo and praised him about how great he was. Then, he immediately caught his feelings of conceit, vanity, and arrogance. He then immediately engaged in the self-struggle of terminating them and transforming them into more positive ones. Arlo was really getting tired from these constant struggles of the fight within himself between dual identities.

IN PRACTICE

The purpose of life is the struggle between the pure identity of soul as created by God and raw ego, which is pumped up falsely by Satan and with which we are constantly deceived. The struggle is to train this raw ego. The soul should be decision maker, but not the ego. The purpose of existence is the life-long struggle between the soul and ego. In this struggle, God is All Merciful. God sent us the scriptures, the prophets, and all the other messengers as guidance and role models for us to define the nature of this struggle and how to win the game.

136. Assumptions & Laws

One day, Erick traveled to another country to visit his friend. The laws and norms of the country were different than the norms and laws in his home country. He was surprised how the laws were so detailed and different in this country, and asked his friend, "Why are the norms and laws in this country so very different than my home country?" His friend said, "In some societies, the norms and accordingly, the laws assume that humans are good, ethical, and moral and accordingly, expect initiatives from people. In some societies, the norms and accordingly, the laws assume that humans are evil, bad, and oppressive and accordingly, protects people from their harms."

IN PRACTICE

Contrasting and comparing different cultures and norms can make a person judgmental about the practices of others. The prophets were not judgmental about other cultures, norms, and teachings. There was an influx of different people from different cultures, understandings, and norms accepting the teachings of the prophets. Yet, the prophets accepted them as they were and taught them the means to connect with God through worship, meditation, practices of individual rights, and justice.

137. Modern Slaves

One day, Dayana traveled to another town to visit her doctor friend. They were very happy to see each other. Although she was with the doctor, the doctor was constantly on her phone—sometimes talking or texting to her patients, or shopping, or engaging herself with social media in different chat groups. Dayana felt uncomfortable. Although her friend was there physically, her mind and emotional states were not present. The doctor constantly had her head down looking at her phone while walking in the house and while outside. She felt bad about her friend. Yet, she seemed to be happy and not care about her engagements.

IN PRACTICE

Mental and emotional slavery can be worse than physical notions of slavery. Our modern slavery hides behind the popular terms of liberty and freedom. Yet, we do not have any self-focus times to engage ourselves with self-accountability. Self-engagements in focus take the person for self-discoveries. True self-discoveries lead the person to God with the reality of 'There is no god but God'. Modern slavery instigates a spiritual disease that 'the world is rotating around me'. This can mean that 'I am so important that if something happens to me everything is going to collapse.' Yet, God mentions in the scriptures often the mortality of all great humans indicating fully the reality of our upcoming demise. Intelligent is the person who focuses on 'There is no god but God'.

138. Self-Destructive Group Identities

One day, Sylvia attended a gathering to benefit herself about collective engagements of spirituality. The lecturer was constantly giving examples of the greatness of her spiritual school. She felt uncomfortable.

IN PRACTICE

Group identities on the spiritual path should come with balance. A person can claim or say, "My group is the best, but it is not the only way." Considering one's spiritual path as the best is normal and expected, so that the person can follow the guidelines on that path from a teacher. Yet, it is wrong to assume and say, "My group is the ONLY way." This implies arrogance, falsehood, and deviation from the true path of God.

139. The Mechanic & The Student

A Harvard religious student named Richard went to a fast food place with his kids since it was Friday and the end of their school week. All of the kids were very happy to eat a nice and yummy chicken hoagie. As they were jumping around in the restaurant and impatiently awaiting their hoagies, there was a religious person from Yemen eating his own food. The two of them did not know each other. While eating, the Yemeni one was chatting with Richard's kids and mentioned that he was a mechanic and fixing the cars. Richard was checking to see if he parked okay on the street, going back and forth watching outside so that he did not get a ticket. The mechanic finished his food and called over to Richard and said, "Please, I want to pay for your food." Richard said, "No, that is okay, thank you." The mechanic insisted so much and Richard accepted it. Then, Richard went to his car and got an expensive gift and gave it to the mechanic. The kids were watching all this. They were amazed and asking questions to understand what was happening. Richard said to himself, "Throw the titles, Harvard, Phds and MDs in the garbage! Be a real man like this person!"

IN PRACTICE

It is very important to be generous. One of the cultures known for their trait of generosity is Yemen. The prophets highly encourage exchanging gifts, feeding each other and being generous so that there is the increase of love between brothers and sisters. In practice, it is more important to embody the traits than the titles. There are a lot of unknown and secret people loved by God. This is the real status and title.

140. Cupping and Going to ER

There were two friends in the mosque. One was trained in cupping. He used to do cupping on people. The other friend used to watch his expert friend while he was cupping others. The expert cupper needed to relocate to another town. One day, an old man came to the temple and said, "I am looking for the expert cupper. I have a lot of back pain." The cupper's friend was there and said, "He moved from here. If you want, I can do it for you. It is not difficult." During the cupping, there was heavy bleeding. The ambulance came and took the old man to the hospital's emergency room. He almost died.

IN PRACTICE

It is important to genuinely learn and apply the spiritual teachings under the guidance and mentorship of a teacher. Sometimes, we cause spiritual deaths on others and on ourselves, but we don't realize it.

BIBLIOGRAPHY

[1] A. Muslim, Sahih Muslim (translated by Siddiqui, A.), Peace Vision, 1972.

[2] D. Parfit, Reasons and Persons, OUP Oxford, 1986, p. 394.

[3] C. Smith, God's Blessings Don't Stop, AuthorHouse, 2014.

[4] M. A. Foust, Loyalty to Loyalty:Josiah Royce and the Genuine Moral Life, Fordham University Press, 2012, p. 26.

[5] J. Carroll Martin, Loving God and Loving Each Other, Xlibris US, 2011, p. 22.

[6] C. Oyler, Actions Speak Louder Than Words Community Activism as Curriculum, Taylor & Francis, 2012.

[7] Y. T. T. Yudha Thianto, The Way to Heaven, Wipf and Stock Publishers, 2014, p. 132.

[8] C. H. Johannes Bauer, Human Fallibility The Ambiguity of Errors for Work and Learning, Springer Netherlands, 2012, p. 64.

[9] B. Lindsay, Jealousy How to Overcome Envy and Competitive Rivalry, Publisher: Self Publisher, 2020.

[10] E. H. Wells, Calmness in times of trouble: a sermon, 2017.

[11] D. Emotion, Strategies to Overcome Stress 10 Ways to Free Yourself from Stress, Negativity, Anxiety and Regain Control of Your Life, Independently Published, 2019, p. 147.

[12] J. Fields, Uncertainty Turning Fear and Doubt Into Fuel for Brilliance, Penguin Publishing Group, 2011.

[13] M. J. Ryan, A Grateful Heart Daily Blessings for the Evening Meals from Buddha to The Beatles, Mango Media, 2011, p. 280.

[14] M. Fleming and D. Worden, Thinking about God and Morality, Pearson Education, 2004, p. 37.

[15] S. Harrogate, Overcome Panic Attacks & Anxiety, CreateSpace Independent Publishing Platform, 2017.

[16] A. E. Kelly, The Psychology of Secrets, Springer US, 2002, p. 10.

GLOSSARY

Accountability: liability; everyone has a free will or agency in this world but accountability for their actions in the afterlife in front of God

Alienating: isolating, separating, disconnecting

Allah: proper name of God in Islam

Allude: explain, refer

Anger: uncontrolled and chaotic human spiritual state

Appreciate: thank

Arrogance: feelings and actions of superiority

Assert: claim

Attribute: adjective, a phrase describing a noun; attributes of God: divine phrases describing God

Authentic: original, genuine, true

Balance: modesty; following the middle way

Behavior: temporary nature of a person

Boost: increase

Compassion: loving and caring

Conscience: internal instinct of distinguishing right or wrong

Consciousness: awareness

Discharge: negative states of spirituality that make the person sad, stressed, and anxious. Emptying oneself from all temporal and worldly positive and negative attachments

Divine: transcendent

Dream: visions when one is sleeping or awake

Ego: self, identifier of a person. Raw and uneducated identifier and controller of a person

Elohim: name of God in Judaism

Endeavor: engagement, activities

Ethical: moral

Etiquette: good manners and respect. Respect in the relationship with God

Evil: anything that causes stress, sadness, or anxiety

Evil eye: the belief of unknown effects of the human eye across different cultures, traditions, and religions. Especially in Sufism, the evil eye effects are due to extreme hatred, jealousy, or, conversely, evil eye effects are due to extreme veneration and love of someone

Expand: enlarge

Experience: internalization of knowledge

Genuine: sincere, original, authentic

Habitual: habit of doing something constantly

Heaven: a place of all maximized pleasures of bodily and spiritual engagements while being with God

Hell: a place of punishment

Humbleness: behavior of modesty in viewing oneself. Accepting the weakness in one's relationship with God and not being disrespectful and arrogant to God

Humility: character or trait of humbleness

Infinite: God, the Unlimited

Intention: planning ideas before the action

Internalize: making it part of one's character, trait, or nature

Intrinsic: internal

Journey: struggles of following guidelines of a mystical school

Knowledge: theoretical understanding of something through education

Meditation: deep focus especially with reflection

Memorization: learning by heart

Mercy: compassion and forgiveness

Mind: logic, reason, and rationality

Miracle: incidents against the law of physics and against all natural sciences

Mosque: temple of Muslims

Mystic: a person who adopts the teachings of mysticism

Mysticism: the knowledge of the transcendent

Notion: concept, idea

One: with capital denoting the one and only Creator

Oppression: unjust action of the strong over the weak

Permanent: constant, not changing, not ending

Pious: devout, practicing

Reliance: dependence

Reward: prize, payment, especially in worldly and afterlife rewards in Islam

Saint: the person believed to be close to God

Scholar: expert, especially in Sufism, the experts who practice what they teach (alim)

Scripture: sacred book or sacred text

Self: ego, identifier of a person; raw and uneducated identifier and controller of a person

Spiritual Journey: struggles of following guidelines of a mystical school

Struggle: efforts to achieve a goal

Surrender: involuntary state of acceptance of the uncontrolled and the unseen

Temple: worship place

Temporal: ending

Temporary: transitory

Temptation: false ideas

Tranquility: peace and calmness

Transcendent: beyond human limits

Unseen: anything five senses cannot testify in scientific methods

ACKNOWLEDGMENTS

I would like to thank all my unnamed teachers, friends, and students for their input, ideas, suggestions, help, and support during and before the preparation of this book.

I would like to thank Ms. Toni Hajdaj for copyediting and proofreading the text. I would like to thank all the Tutumlu Family members and Ms. Sumaya and Zahra K. during the preparation of the text.

Lastly, I would like to thank all of my family members for their patience with me during the preparation of this book.

AUTHOR BIO

Dr. Yunus J. Kumek is currently teaching at Harvard Divinity School and also, in sociology department at State University of New York (SUNY) Buffalo State. He has been religious studies coordinator at State University of New York (SUNY) Buffalo State. Before becoming interested in religious studies, Dr. Kumek was doing his doctorate degree in physics at SUNY at Buffalo published academic papers in the areas of quantum physics, and medical physics. He has then decided to engage with the world of social sciences through social anthropology, education, and cultural anthropology in his doctorate studies and later spent a few more years as a research associate in the anthropology department of the same university. Recently, he completed a postdoctoral fellowship at Harvard Divinity school and published books on religious literacy through ethnography and practical mysticism: Sufi journeys of heart and mind. Dr. Kumek, who remains interested in physics—solves physics problems to relax—enjoys different languages, German, Spanish, Arabic, Hebrew, Urdu, and Turkish, especially in his research of scriptural and theological analysis. Dr. Kumek takes great pleasure in classical poetry as well.

INDEX

Made in the USA
Monee, IL
30 August 2021